Twayne's United States Authors Series

Sylvia E. Bowman, *Editor*

INDIANA UNIVERSITY

John Steinbeck

JOHN STEINBECK

By WARREN FRENCH
Kansas State University

 2

Twayne Publishers, Inc.   ::   New York

for
PHILIP GRAHAM
of the
University of Texas
from an
involuntary expatriate

Preface

JOHN STEINBECK is not critically fashionable today. He is not so often mentioned respectfully in discussions of American fiction as Faulkner, Hemingway, and Fitzgerald; if the will of some literary historians prevailed, he would be relegated to a footnote.

It is encouraging, therefore, that the major works of Steinbeck remain in print in inexpensive editions, which continue to multiply here and abroad. Even more heartening, since nothing in the long run is more important to the health of literature than getting young people enthusiastic about it, is the surge of excitement observable in students reading Steinbeck carefully for the first time.

Why this curiously divided reaction to Steinbeck? It is partly the result of a curious critical ill-logic. Undeniably Steinbeck's novels since World War II have failed to live up to his earlier works. Since possible reasons for this deterioration will be discussed in the book, I wish only here to point out that by "reverse reasoning," the weakness of these later books is supposed in some way to justify revising downward the estimates of the earlier. The talents of other authors, especially ones of a Romantic temperament, like Wordsworth and Emerson flagged; yet we do not find the vital works of their youth disregarded as literary landmarks. Like all books, Steinbeck's great stories of the thirties must be judged on their own merits.

Some critics have always been suspicious of these merits. Some do not like Steinbeck because he does not see the world as they see it and does not tell them what they wish to hear. It is critically fashionable today to be "disengaged," which means that one accepts the advantages of civilization and declines responsibility for its other aspects. The less hope a writer sees for civilization, the more fashionable he is likely to be. Liberalism, since it is blamed for the sins of its opponents, is distrusted and denounced. Steinbeck is condemned for not being Kafka or Becket. Possibly Kafka is right, but Steinbeck may be too; the truth may be complex. A criticism that insists on seeing Steinbeck as not-Kafka never sees him as himself.

Steinbeck's reputation has also suffered because his novels are easy to read. He often fuses a lucid realistic narrative with a symbolic statement about man's condition. The surface narratives, however, are so smoothly executed that people do not read them carefully and miss what lies beneath. When one encounters a work like *Finnegan's Wake* or *The Balcony,* for example, one knows he must look below the surface for the meaning. The discovery that books with deep symbolic meanings are often very difficult to read then leads to the fallacious assumption that the obverse is true: ones that are easy to read do not have deep symbolic meanings. Since we do not read them carefully, we underrate masterpieces like *The Beggar's Opera* and Saki's stories, and we assume that our shortcomings are theirs.

The object of *John Steinbeck* is to get people to read as carefully as they should these deceptively lucid works and not to dismiss them with secondhand generalizations. Another object is to point out specifically the universal applicability of the observations in many of Steinbeck's novels and thus answer criticisms that have attempted to rationalize a distaste for Steinbeck's indifference to partisan feeling by dismissing as purely regional the problems he stresses.

A novel-by-novel analysis of Steinbeck's works will be most useful, however, if attention is first called to the three general tendencies that have done most to shape his fiction.

The first of these is his tendency to write allegorically. Allegory is, of course, the ancient art of discussing one thing, especially an unfamiliar or abstract concept, by talking about something familiar that stands for the unfamiliar. The best known allegories are the fables of Aesop and the parables of Christ, which embody much of the traditional wisdom of the two principal intellectual currents that mingle in Western thought; but it is really doubtful whether any enduring work of art does not have some allegorical significance. Allegory, nevertheless, is distrusted in the twentieth century; and an increasing amount of literature strives to be merely unfocused reporting—just as an increasing amount of painting is non-objective.

The difference between the reporter and the allegorist is that the reporter seeks simply to collect facts whereas the allegorist looks for a pattern in the event around which an account of it may be organized. A reporter is concerned with what makes an event unique, while an allegorist is concerned with what makes it typical of recurrent patterns of human behavior.

Steinbeck, however, is a marked contrast to many allegorists whose art has been at the service of an entrenched theology; for the second important thing about him is his preoccupation with non-teleological thinking. Just how this form of scientific thinking operates cannot be briefly explained; Steinbeck, with the help of his friend Ed Ricketts, tried to clarify its characteristics in the fourteenth chapter of *The Sea of Cortez;* and one should turn there for an account of his concept. The key idea is perhaps that "non-teleological thinking concerns itself primarily not with what should be, or could be, or might be, but rather with what actually *'is'*—attempting at most to answer the already sufficiently difficult questions *what* or *how,* instead of *why.*" Theologians (religious, economic, political) especially resist this form of thinking because it excludes any consideration of first causes, predestined goals, or special providences and because it may cast doubt upon their priestly authority.

Differences arising from teleological and non-teleological approaches have been at the root of many quarrels between science and theology; yet even the scientist cannot be entirely non-theological if he is to do anything at all. Since he cannot hope to observe everything that *is,* he must choose to observe some phenomena at the expense of others. As soon as he makes a selection, he opens himself to the question, "Why did you choose this instead of that?" Even if he answers only, "I prefer this to that," he expresses faith in a pleasure principle. Even the non-teleological thinker, in short, must choose a theology (even if just a consistent opposition to any other theology) to give his work direction.

Steinbeck's theology—the third important thing to remember about him—accords remarkably with that of the nineteenth-century American transcendentalists. It is even more difficult to define transcendentalism than non-teleological thought; it is perhaps enough to say here that it is a set of imprecise, idealistic doctrines that demand that man be both intensely individualistic and selflessly altruistic at the same time. The best way to learn about transcendentalism is to read the three major documents of the movement—Emerson's Essays (especially "Self-Reliance"), Thoreau's *Walden*, especially the first and last chapters, and Walt Whitman's *Leaves of Grass*. Steinbeck's "faith" might, in fact, best be summarized by a single line in Whitman's "By Blue Ontario's Shore": "How dare you place any thing before a man?" An insistence on the primacy of human dignity is the force that has kept Steinbeck from committing himself to some Cause.

Whether the transcendentalists specifically influenced Steinbeck lies outside the scope of this book; the point is that transcendental ideas have been fairly widespread among intellectuals in this country and have come to be regarded as constituting a characteristically American philosophy of life. Steinbeck's enthusiasm for these ideas, therefore, gives him a place in the development of a distinctive and distinguished American tradition.

These three characteristics of Steinbeck's thought have had obvious effects upon his artistic successes and failures. When his personal experience has provided him with engrossing material, his propensity for allegory has provided a plan, his non-teleological thought a capacity for detachment, and his transcendental idealism a vigorous compassion that makes works like *The Red Pony* and *The Grapes of Wrath* both socially and artistically significant. On the other hand, when he has dealt with contrived material, the allegory clogs the narrative, the non-teleological effort at detachment seems merely carelessness or contempt, and the transcendental idealism becomes bombastic sentimentality.

In order to concentrate on the allegorical, non-teleological, and transcendental characteristics of Steinbeck's work within the format of this series, I have omitted discussion of other undeniably important topics already adequately treated in Peter Lisca's *The Wide World of John Steinbeck* and in the essays in Tedlock and Wicker's *Steinbeck and His Critics*.

University of Florida   WARREN FRENCH

Acknowledgments

Grateful acknowledgment is made to the Viking Press, Inc., for permission to use throughout this volume quotations from these copyrighted works of John Steinbeck: *Burning Bright, Cannery Row, Cup of Gold, East of Eden, The Forgotten Village, The Grapes of Wrath, In Dubious Battle, The Long Valley, The Moon is Down, Of Mice and Men, Once There Was a War, The Pastures of Heaven, The Pearl, A Russian Journal, The Log from the Sea of Cortez, The Short Reign of Pippin IV, Sweet Thursday, To a God Unknown, Tortilla Flat, The Wayward Bus.*

Quotations throughout this volume from Peter Lisca, *The Wide World of John Steinbeck*, copyright 1958 by Rutgers, the State University of New Jersey, appear through the courtesy of the Trustees of the University and Mr. William Sloane, Director of the Rutgers Press. I also wish to thank Charles Scribner's Sons, publishers, for permission to quote from F. Scott Fitzgerald's *The Great Gatsby;* the Houghton Mifflin Company, publishers, for permission to quote from Maxwell Geismar's *Writers in Crisis;* and the University of Minnesota Press for permission to quote from Charles C. Walcutt's *American Literary Naturalism: A Divided Stream*, copyright 1956.

Quotations from the review columns of *The New Yorker* and *Time* magazines are used through the kind consent of their publishers, and quotations from John Steinbeck's "Critics, Critics, Burning Bright" appear through the courtesy of the author and the *Saturday Review*.

Contents

Chronology

1902   Born Salinas, California, February 27.

1919   Graduated from Salinas High School.

1920   Enrolled at Stanford.

1924   Published stories in the Stanford *Spectator*.

1925   Left Stanford permanently without degree; visited New York City; worked for the *American* (newspaper).

1929   *Cup of Gold*.

1930   Married Carol Henning; moved to Pacific Grove.

1932   *The Pastures of Heaven*.

1933   *To a God Unknown;* "The Red Pony" in *North American Review*.

1934   "The Murder" in *O. Henry Prize Stories*.

1935   *Tortilla Flat* (Commonwealth Club of California Gold Medal).

1936   *In Dubious Battle* (Commonwealth Club of California Gold Medal); "The Harvest Gypsies" in San Francisco *News*.

1937   *Of Mice and Men* (novel and play—Drama Critics' Circle Award); chosen one of the ten outstanding young men of the year.

1938   *The Long Valley; Their Blood is Strong*.

1939   *The Grapes of Wrath* (Pulitzer Prize).

1940   Visited Gulf of California with Ed Ricketts; filmed *The Forgotten Village* in Mexico (book published in 1941).

1941   *The Sea of Cortez;* films of *Of Mice and Men* and *The Grapes of Wrath*.

1942   *Bombs Away; The Moon is Down* (novel and play); divorced from Carol Henning.

1943   Married Gwyn Verdon; visited the European war zone for the New York *Herald Tribune.*

1944   *Lifeboat* (film).

1945   *Cannery Row;* "The Pearl of the World"; *A Medal for Benny* (film); bought home in New York.

1947   *The Pearl* (book and film); *The Wayward Bus;* trip to Russia.

1948   *A Russian Journal,* with Robert Capa; divorced from Gwyn Verdon; Ed Ricketts died.

1949   *The Red Pony* (film).

1950   *Burning Bright* (novel and play); *Viva Zapata!* (film); married Elaine Scott.

1952   *East of Eden;* sent reports to *Collier's* from Europe.

1954   *Sweet Thursday.*

1955   *Pipe Dream* (Richard Rodgers and Oscar Hammerstein II musical comedy based on *Sweet Thursday*); editorials for *Saturday Review.*

1957   *The Short Reign of Pippin IV.*

1958   *Once There Was a War.*

John Steinbeck

CHAPTER 1

The Man Behind the Books

JOHN STEINBECK used to loathe publicity. During the 1950's he relaxed his self-imposed silence and discussed his activities and ideas in national magazines, but he still shied away from questions about his family and friends. He wishes to speak through his books, and it is to them we must turn to learn about him. Unquestionably more will be known in the future about Steinbeck and the motives behind his writing. For the present, however, we must rely upon the public record—especially upon the long biographical sketch, prepared in 1957 by Peter Lisca for E. W. Tedlock, Jr., and C. V. Wicker's anthology, *Steinbeck and His Critics*, which was checked by the novelist and his wife.

What we already know of Steinbeck enables us to see that his life has fallen into three main divisions, as he suggests in his longest autobiographical essay, "The Making of a New Yorker";[1] and it is into these three divisions that I shall sort "the facts" about him. Some of these need scrutinizing, since Steinbeck, like Sir Henry Morgan in *Cup of Gold,* is prone to romanticize and aggrandize himself. I have labeled reports that may prove apocryphal.

I *The Aspiring Californian*

The two important facts about the first phase of Steinbeck's life are that he was a Californian and that he wanted to be a serious writer. His birthplace could have inspired him. There is something special about the Golden State beyond the legends fostered by its Chambers of Commerce. A big, beautiful land, it was, and as Steinbeck and other writers have emphasized, the last frontier. Epics might be written about the tumultuous episodes in its history—the dispossession of the sedentary Spanish settlers, the Gold Rush, the struggles of the railroad empire-builders, the San Francisco disaster, the troubles with migrant laborers and imported minority groups. Many of its writers—Frank Norris, Gertrude Atherton, Stewart Edward White, Upton Sinclair, Robinson Jeffers—have called for and sought to produce an American epic.

Steinbeck, when he has written of the problems that confront man in his epical struggle with unreliable nature and his own uncontrollable passions, has not been unique in his own country, but a contributor to a vigorous tradition. His break with this regional tradition has had a disturbing effect upon his career; it has also, in the absence of a successor of comparable stature, had a disturbing effect upon the state's cultural pretensions.

Unlike other celebrators of the new El Dorado, Steinbeck is a native Californian and a descendant of the conquerors of the frontier. His maternal grandfather left Ireland to settle in the Salinas Valley, and his father migrated from Florida at the time of the Civil War. The writer's family has been active in public life: John Ernst, Sr., his father, was not only a miller, but for many years the treasurer of Monterey County; and his mother, Olive Hamilton (a character in *East of Eden*) taught school at several places, including Big Sur, site of an artists' colony later made famous by Henry Miller. One of three children (the others, girls), Steinbeck was born February 27, 1902, in the small agricultural trading center of Salinas.

As a child, he had ample access to the three things Emerson said went into the making of a scholar; nature, books, action. He heeded, intentionally or not, Emerson's injunctions about the roles of each. Although a small-town boy, Steinbeck lived close to the country and has apparently drawn upon his own experiences for *The Red Pony* and other works with farm settings. He read widely, too; Peter Lisca quotes his mentioning an early acquaintance with Dostoevsky, Milton, Flaubert, George Eliot, Thomas Hardy, and especially Malory, whose *Morte d'Arthur* Steinbeck has described as not only the first book he owned but the one that had, except possibly for the King James version of the Bible, the greatest influence on his work.

He was not, however, to be tyrannized by books; he wrote for high school and college papers in Salinas and at Stanford, but could never bring himself to complete the rituals prescribed for obtaining an academic degree. During the five years in the twenties that he sporadically attended Stanford, he also was more active than perhaps even Emerson dreamed of a writer being. He worked on ranches, joined a road-building gang, worked in the laboratory of a sugar-beet factory, and even helped build Madison Square Garden.

He held this last job when, after leaving Stanford in 1925, he made his first trip to New York to attempt to establish himself as a writer. This unsuccessful venture he discusses in "The Making of a New Yorker," reporting that for a while he did work for the old New York *American* (a defunct newspaper), but balked at a girl's suggestion that he enter the advertising business before trying to earn a living by creative writing. Although he had printed only five satirical poems and stories in undergraduate journals at Stanford, Steinbeck was encouraged by an editor for the Robert McBride Company to prepare a book of short stories. When this manuscript was rejected, the disgruntled writer went back to California to work on novels while employed as, among other things, caretaker for a lodge high in the Sierras near Lake Tahoe.

Steinbeck had prepared and apparently circulated a number of manuscripts before his historical extravaganza, *Cup of Gold* —a pseudo-epic about a "lost generation" version of Sir Henry Morgan, a seventeenth-century Caribbean pirate—was published by the company that had rejected his short stories. The novel appeared in 1929 just two months before the stock market crash ended a carefree era. Lewis Gannett reports in a preface for a new edition of the novel in 1936 that 1,533 copies were sold but the few newspaper critics who reviewed it refused to take it seriously.

After making several false starts, Steinbeck produced the first and still one of the best of his California novels, *The Pastures of Heaven*. But books moved slowly in the depression year of 1932, and the first two publishing houses to handle the book went out of business before finishing the binding of the edition. Unbound copies were still on hand in 1936, when the market for Steinbeck's work improved. He reports that he received four hundred dollars for the novel and that this was even more than he received for his first and third works, which failed to repay the publishers' two-hundred-and-fifty-dollar advances.

Between the publication of his first two novels Steinbeck had been married for the first time to Carol Henning, a San Jose girl with whom he had eloped to Los Angeles. The newly-weds moved to the quiet, respectable Methodist settlement of Pacific Grove (often the butt of Steinbeck's ridicule), where his father provided them with a small house and twenty-five dollars a month, enough to exist on during the depths of the depression when many people, like the *paisanos* of Tortilla Flat, had to live mainly on good nature. While living in Pacific Grove, Steinbeck met one of the people who was to have the greatest influence on his life and work, Ed Ricketts, the proprietor of a biological supply laboratory on Monterey's Cannery Row, who was to serve the author as friend, advisor, collaborator, and model for the heroes of "The Snake," *Cannery Row,* and *Sweet Thursday.*

Steinbeck moved to Los Angeles in 1932, but very soon returned to the Monterey peninsula before the publication in 1933 of his third novel, *To a God Unknown,* an involved and generally unsuccessful allegory that Harry Moore, one of Steinbeck's earliest critics, thinks caused the failure of Robert O. Ballou and left Steinbeck without a publisher. The author's only consolation in that dark year was his finally selling the first two parts of *The Red Pony* and several other short stories to the *North American Review.* When "The Murder" was selected as an O. Henry prize story in 1934, Steinbeck achieved his first national recognition. His days of obscurity were just about over; the next year this writer, who had never expected any of his books to sell well and who had once said he hoped for an audience of about twenty thousand, found himself inadvertently a celebrity.

II *The California Celebrity*

The auspicious event that inaugurated the second phase of Steinbeck's career was the publication of *Tortilla Flat,* the droll pseudo-Arthurian investigation of Monterey's idlers that Steinbeck apparently regarded as a relaxation from the taxing labors on *To a God Unknown*. *Tortilla Flat* had a hard time finding a publisher, for editors found the story too frivolous for trying times. Steinbeck's change in fortune is generally attributed to the promotional activities of Ben Abramson, an astute Chicago bookman, who insisted that Pascal Covici read two novels of Steinbeck's with which he was not familiar. Covici was reportedly as fascinated with *The Pastures of Heaven* as Abramson; sought further works by its author; read the *Tortilla Flat* manuscript; and published it under the Covici, Friede imprint. Steinbeck had found at last the editor and publisher who was to sponsor all of his major works.

Tortilla Flat's reception was mixed; socially conscious critics missed its ironic humor and attacked it as a sentimental defense of vagabondage. The readers, however, liked it, as they had James Thurber's *My Life and Hard Times;* and the novel won the Gold Medal of the Commonwealth Club of San Francisco for the year's best by a Californian. Best of all, from Steinbeck's viewpoint, *Tortilla Flat* was purchased by Hollywood for a sum variously reported as three or four thousand dollars. Although the film rights changed hands several times and the novel was not actually filmed for almost a decade (when a mangled version starring Spencer Tracy failed to do either justice to the story or impressive business), this was the most money Steinbeck had ever earned. He has several times remarked about the effect of such a fortune upon a man accustomed to living on thirty-five dollars a week.

There were several discernible effects. He wrote no more of the short, satirical verses that he had contributed in January, 1935, to the Monterey *Beacon*, but intensified the seriousness of his work. He made a long-planned trip to Mexico, but found he could not work there and returned, according to Harry Moore, to a new home in Los Gatos, California.

In 1936, one of his busiest years, he published *In Dubious Battle*—an ambiguous analysis of a strike—that became, as he predicted, the center of a storm of critical controversy. Opinions ranged from Mary McCarthy's snide and shrill denunciation in the *Nation* of the style and substance to Peter Quennell's appreciation in *New Statesman and Nation* of Steinbeck's non-commitment. His work now in demand, Steinbeck also placed short stories in *Esquire* and *Harper's;* and the seed for *The Grapes of Wrath* was sown when he was commissioned to write a series of articles for the San Francisco *News* about conditions in California's migrant labor camps.

Steinbeck's stock climbed in 1937. The reception of *Of Mice and Men* was the best that had greeted one of his works; only the *Nation's* critic was unimpressed. The powerful little fable was selected by the Book-of-the-Month Club, which meant the immediate sale of 75,000 copies. Steinbeck, who a scant three years earlier might have been considered a failure, was selected one of the Ten Outstanding Young Men of the Year. Flushed with success, he returned to New York in triumph and was depressed by a formal dinner for Thomas Mann. After touring England, Ireland, Sweden, and Russia, he returned to this country in the autumn to retire to Bucks County, just then becoming a fashionable retreat, to work on the script of the play version of *Of Mice and Men* at the home of and with the assistance of the famous playwright and play-doctor, George Kaufman.

The play opened to laudatory reviews during the Thanksgiving season; and Steinbeck, already well known in literary circles, became a celebrity. Although *Of Mice and Men* lost the Pulitzer Prize to Thornton Wilder's *Our Town*, it won the New York Drama Critic Circle's award on the first ballot and enjoyed a long run before becoming a much-talked-about motion picture. Steinbeck could just about write his own ticket, but his success was not contagious. Jack Kirkland failed to capitalize on it when, looking for a successor to the long-running *Tobacco Road*, he tried a vulgar dramatization of *Tortilla Flat* that failed within a week.

Still as high-minded as some of his characters, Steinbeck turned down an offer from *Life* to do a series about the migrant laborers, because he could not make money from their plight; even he, however, was not able to avoid the fortune he was to make from his novel about them. He was collecting material for this work even as the play *Of Mice and Men* went into production in New York. The night it opened he was living in a migrant camp—having followed its inhabitants across country from Oklahoma—and working on a satirical novel tentatively entitled *L'affaire Lettuceberg* that was to be transformed into *The Grapes of Wrath*. He also contributed new material to a pamphlet in which his earlier stories for the San Francisco *News* were collected by the Simon J. Lubin Society of California under the title *Their Blood is Strong.*

Steinbeck's improving fortunes were not enough to stave off disaster for his publisher. Covici's partner, Donald Friede, had already drifted off to Hollywood to become an agent; in August, 1938, while *The Long Valley*—the collection of short stories Steinbeck had long waited to see published—was in proof and while the author was working on the manuscript of his greatest success, the chief creditors took over the house of Covici, Friede. Steinbeck and his discoverer did not, however, part company: a desirable property for any publisher, Steinbeck chose to follow Covici when the latter became an executive editor for the Viking Press. *The Long Valley* was the first of many of Steinbeck's books to bear this firm's imprint.

In 1939 the publishers discovered what a treasure they had acquired. Had it not been for the furor a few years earlier over the publication of Margaret Mitchell's *Gone With the Wind,* it would be no exaggeration to call the appearance of *The Grapes of Wrath* the publishing event of the decade. Although critics and public alike generally missed the point of the book which they compared to *Uncle Tom's Cabin,* they made up in enthusiasm what they lacked in perceptiveness by buying printing after printing. *Publisher's Weekly* listed the novel as the top seller of 1939 and the eighth best one of 1940; Frank Luther Mott estimates in *Golden Multitudes* that well over half a million copies of the original edition were sold. Libraries had waiting lists months long. Steinbeck won the Pulitzer Prize for the best novel of the year, along with the American Booksellers' Award; and, on the strength of the tremendous impact of this work, he was elected to membership in the National Institute of Arts and Letters.

There are no public estimates of the novel's total earnings; but there have been several American editions, numerous foreign editions and translations, and the story was purchased by Twentieth-Century-Fox and made into one of the great social-protest films. Some indication of the improvement in Steinbeck's income can, however, be gathered from the report that his first wife received a $220,000 settlement at the time of their divorce in 1942. It has also been estimated that, at the time he became affiliated with the Viking Press, his books had earned a total of approximately $50,000. He had at least become affluent enough to afford the generous gesture of giving his thousand-dollar Pulitzer Prize money to Richard Lovejoy, a Monterey department store executive, to start him on a literary career.

Steinbeck was not during the next two decades to occupy the eminent position he did at the time the book and film versions of *The Grapes of Wrath* were being deservedly hailed as outstanding examples of pre-war trends in their *genres*. He became a favorite of not only the public, but the great. He became friendly enough with President Roosevelt to call at the White House and even, he reminisced in an article for *Collier's,* to suggest a plan for harassing the Nazis with counterfeit money that delighted the President but shocked Secretary of the Treasury Morgenthau.[2]

Generally, however, he avoided the spotlight. Late in 1939 when the excitement generated by *The Grapes of Wrath* made him of sufficient literary significance to be the subject of a pioneering critical monograph, Harry T. Moore's *The Novels of John Steinbeck*, he took off with Ed Ricketts on a marine biological expedition to the coastal regions north of San Francisco. In March, 1940, he accompanied his friend on another expedition to the Gulf of California; this trip is described in *Sea of Cortez,* which also contains an account of the non-teleological philosophy that attracted both men. In April Steinbeck returned to Mexico to make a semi-documentary film, *The Forgotten Village,* about the struggle to introduce modern medicine in a backward community. This work kept him busy the rest of the year. His travels, however, had exasperated his wife, who in 1942 sued for divorce on the grounds that she was too much alone at Pacific Grove.

That same year Steinbeck was on the road again; for he was commissioned by the Army Air Force to write a promotional book about its training program (many Americans, especially parents, still feared flying). *Bombs Away,* although frankly propaganda and not the success Steinbeck's recent novels had been, was worth $250,000 to Hollywood and to the Air Forces Aid Society, to which Steinbeck turned over all royalties. Meanwhile, the author had already made his major fictional contribution to the war effort: the play-novelette, *The Moon is Down*.

Although both versions of this apparently hurriedly written work, which reached Broadway in April, 1942, were sympathetically received and although the King of Norway subsequently decorated Steinbeck for the contribution of the work to the liberation movement, it won no major literary awards. The general opinion was that it was far less effective than *Of Mice and Men* had been, principally because of the author's remoteness from his material. Hollywood, nevertheless, which can reward richly if sometimes belatedly, paid $300,000 for the right to make an unremarkable picture of the work. Steinbeck's most effective fictional treatment of the problems posed by the war is actually his script for Alfred Hitchcock's film, *Lifeboat*, a complex allegory of a world adrift that owed its success when it was released early in 1944 less to its controversial symbolism than to the exertions of Tallulah Bankhead. Unfortunately, the script has never been published.

Work on this project completed, Steinbeck decided to acquaint himself at first hand with our fighting forces and spent from June to December, 1943, with the troops in the European Theatre as a special correspondent for the New York *Herald Tribune*. Apparently he had planned a novel about the war, but Peter Lisca reports in *The Wide World of John Steinbeck* that the writer was "too disheartened by what he had seen of the war to prolong the experience in any way and he decided not to publish it." Even the human interest stories he sent home were not collected until 1958.

Rather than concentrate upon the war, he nostalgically turned to an attempt to recapture in *Cannery Row* the life with Ed Ricketts in the thirties before Steinbeck had become a celebrity and the world had gone mad. *Cannery Row* is an artistic triumph, a far better work than is generally acknowledged, but it is also an elegy. With it, the California phase of Steinbeck's career ended, although it was some time before the public or even the writer himself was aware of this. His rejection of the overwhelming problem of trying to make artistic sense out of the war marked also both a literal and symbolic passage from the innocence of California's valleys to the sophisticated city.

III *The New Yorker*

Steinbeck never returned to California to live after his first divorce. Although he spent some time in Hollywood working on motion picture versions of his own books and other works, he lost contact with the people who had provided him with the material for his most enduring novels. The circumstances of his second marriage to Gwyn Verdon on March 29, 1943, suggest his changed environment; the ceremony occurred in the patio of the writer Lyle Saxon's home in the French Quarter of New Orleans and the small group present included Paul de Kruif, the famous scientific writer. The period of this second marriage is the most obscure in Steinbeck's career; he intensified his efforts to escape public notice and apparently tried to live the life of a private citizen in two brownstone houses at 175-77 East 78th Street, Manhattan, that he purchased in November, 1945. During this marriage, Steinbeck's only children, Tom and John, were born. Although these boys are occasionally mentioned in Steinbeck's writings (one is the central figure in the frequently reprinted "How to Tell Good Guys from Bad Guys"), he has made even more strenuous efforts to keep them out of the public eye than he has to protect himself.

During this period, Steinbeck reports, he had the experience of feeling that he had become a New Yorker, a thing he was glad of because of the privacy and the perfect freedom to be one's self that the big city offered. He did not entirely drop from public notice, though, for he was considered in 1945 for the Nobel Prize for literature, which was won by the Chilean poetess, Gabriela Mistral. Nor was he idle. He expanded a legend he had mentioned in *Sea of Cortez* into a piece for the *Woman's Home Companion*. Two years later, it became *The Pearl,* a short book and a beautifully made Mexican film. He worked hard, too, on *The Wayward Bus,* but this first major postwar novel failed to jell; and, although a Book-of-the-Month Club selection, it never really attracted much attention. In 1947 he made a trip to Russia with his friend, the photographer Robert Capa, that provided material for *A Russian Journal,* a beautifully written and illustrated book that also failed to appeal to the public.

A high note of 1948 was Steinbeck's election to the American

Academy of Arts and Letters, the "inner sanctum" of the National Institute. But he fared less well in private life. Without publicity, he was divorced from Gwyn Verdon; and he lost his most admired associate when Ed Ricketts was killed in an automobile accident. Perhaps to escape personal concerns, he threw himself into writing for the mass media. He planned to organize with Capa (later killed while on a photographic mission in Viet Nam) a television producing firm; and he went to Hollywood, where he saw *The Red Pony* sympathetically filmed and then worked until 1950 on the script for Marlon Brando's portrayal of a Mexican Revolutionary hero, *Viva Zapata!*

In 1950 came the *Burning Bright* debacle. Steinbeck's third play-novelette was simply dismissed by literary critics and failed after thirteen performances on Broadway, although produced by the usually magical combination of Rodgers and Hammerstein. For the first time an obviously hurt Steinbeck replied to his critics with a moving, but not entirely justified, defense of his play in the *Saturday Review*. His stock as a public figure was at about its lowest point when on December 29, 1950, he married Elaine Scott, former wife of film star Zachary Scott, at the New York home of his publisher, Harold K. Guinzburg.

Steinbeck's third marriage brought him out of his shell. While working on his second big novel, *East of Eden,* he prepared the highly personal tribute to his friend Ed Ricketts to be published in 1951 in a new edition of *The Log from the Sea of Cortez*. He also formed some sort of association with *Collier's* magazine; for in April, 1952, he began, with an account of his verbal battle with Italian Communists, a series of articles about a European trip he had made while collecting material for a book, parts of which, he announced, *Collier's* would publish. He was photographed with his wife for the first article, and pictures she had taken were used with another. The projected book, however, has never materialized.

Also in 1952 *East of Eden,* an attempt to re-create the history of his native region, was unenthusiastically received by most critics, who felt that too much had been attempted. There was more enthusiasm for a collection of six of his earlier short novels the next year, but very little for *Sweet Thursday* in 1954. This ill-advised attempt to return to Cannery Row was turned into a Rodgers and Hammerstein musical comedy under the title *Pipe Dream,* but not even the singing of Helen Traubel kept it alive beyond its first season. A more dismal failure was the project called *The Best of Steinbeck,* which failed to reach New York. Steinbeck fared better in the films: Elia Kazan turned the last section of *East of Eden* into a vehicle for the screen debut in 1955 of the teen-age idol, James Dean, while Jayne Mansfield attracted spectators to a mediocre version of *The Wayward Bus* in 1957.

During this period Steinbeck was writing for a number of magazines, including *Holiday.* He began in 1955 to write editorials for the *Saturday Review,* but most of these pleasant, highly generalized statements are little more than potboilers. Most of Steinbeck's work during the fifties was superficial journalism, like the introductions to a collection of Adlai Stevenson's 1952 campaign speeches and to selections from the works of Al Capp, creator of "Li'l Abner."

Two exceptions are the short story "How Mr. Hogan Robbed a Bank," in the *Atlantic Monthly* (March, 1956) and the novel, *The Short Reign of Pippin IV* (1957), both of which suggest that Steinbeck might be finding his way to a new satirical style. Unfortunately there has been no successor to these works in three years. Steinbeck has talked since 1955 of a "big book" he is working on, but he has broken his silence recently only to jibe at American complacency in *Coronet* and *Esquire.* He may still produce a significant novel, but I make no predictions. The best Steinbeck books of the last part of the fifties are about him—Tedlock and Wicker's collection of critical essays about his work and Peter Lisca's comprehensive analysis of his career, *The Wide World of John Steinbeck.* As the sixties begin, Steinbeck seems a man more written about than writing.

CHAPTER 2

Gatsby Sails the Caribbean

IF STEINBECK later had not written better novels, *Cup of Gold*, his first published book, would surely be as deservedly forgotten as most of the 10,186 others Lewis Gannett says were published in the same end-of-the-boom year of 1929.[1] It is difficult to speak well of the novel. The dialogue is stilted; the characters, two-dimensional; the style, pretentious; the tone, inconsistent; the plot, awkwardly managed; the theme, confused. Yet one cannot ignore it since it is important both as a symbol of its era and as a portent of the author's future. Steinbeck struggled in it with ideas he was later to treat masterfully.

Since *Cup of Gold* is not likely to be widely read, a discussion of its relation to Steinbeck's later work should be prefaced with the explanation that it concerns a Welsh farmlad who hankers to go to sea. After a strange recluse with the Arthurian name of Merlin predicts that this young Henry Morgan may become a great man, the lad sails for the West Indies, where, through the duplicity of his ship's master, he becomes for four years the indentured servant of a man who educates him and treats him like a son. Given his freedom, Henry announces that he must be off to the bounding main; and, after being snubbed by titled relatives in Jamaica, he buys the captaincy of a pirate ship with funds filched from his trusting master.

The young pirate is fantastically successful; and many small ventures lead to his final attack upon Panama City, the "Cup of Gold" of the title and the great and supposedly invulnerable Spanish treasure-house. The attack succeeds, but the scene of Morgan's greatest triumph is also the scene of his most crushing personal defeat which is administered by "La Santa

Roja," a legendary beauty of whom all men dream. Although
unlucky in love, Morgan soars to new heights when he cheats
his piratical collaborators of their share of Panama's fabulous
loot and, apparently single-handedly, sails a galleon back to
Jamaica, where he sinks into respectability as lieutenant-
governor and henpecked husband of his snobbish cousin,
Elizabeth.

Peter Lisca in *The Wide World of John Steinbeck* describes
this lurid tale as a Faust legend, but I cannot agree. In the first
place the book is too carelessly constructed to be a consistent
allegory; if it had been completely thought out, something
would have come of Morgan's early promise to Merlin to "come
back [to Cambria] when I am whole again," but nothing does—
the matter is never even mentioned again. The principal elements of a Faust legend are, furthermore, the making of an
unnatural pact and the attempt to escape its consequences.
Morgan, like Faust, is disillusioned when he obtains the power
he has dreamed of; but so are many Romantic heroes. Morgan
makes no pacts with supernatural powers nor does he attempt
to escape the destruction of his illusions; he is, in fact, quite
comfortable in the hell of Jamaican officialdom. There is no
indication, furthermore, that Morgan, like the various Fausts,
is consigned to either heaven or hell; for him there is simply
"no light anywhere." Objecting to a Faustian interpretation of
the novel is not merely quibbling; for the Faust figure, who
would sacrifice the natural order to his lust for personal power,
is the very one that Steinbeck has consistently been unable to
realize artistically to the detriment of such works as *The
Moon is Down.*

Definitely present in the novel, however, are echoes of the
Arthurian quest for the Holy Grail. What fascinated Steinbeck
about the pirate Henry Morgan is not clear, but his Welsh
origins and the references to Arthurian legends early in the
book tempt one to seek a more consistent allegory than one
finds. The title indicates that Panama City is indeed a kind
of grail for Morgan, but about all this hero has in common with
the knights of the Round Table is an overpowering vision and
a strong arm. It is also true that Morgan hurls away an actual
golden cup with an obviously religio-sexual significance; but,

if his rejection means anything, it can only be interpreted as an attempt to escape both primitive innocence and sophistication and steer a middle course of superficial conformity that would scandalize knights-errant.

Certainly Morgan is more nearly an anti-Arthurian than an Arthurian symbol. The Grail disappears from the story, but not as in *Morte d'Arthur* because "he is not served nor worshipped to his right by them of this land, for they be turned to evil living." It is hurled aside into a pile of diamonds when the hero finds post-Freudian self-analysis more absorbing than what the cup symbolizes. Of course, it may have been Steinbeck's intent to write an anti-Arthurian story; we shall find him insisting in *Tortilla Flat* and *In Dubious Battle* that the days of chivalry are over, if indeed the selfless knight was not always the kind of myth that ante-bellum culture and the noble outlaw of the frontier became.

Morgan's introspection provides the clue to the legend that *Cup of Gold* really parallels. If we strip away historical trappings, the baroque language, and the tropical undergrowth, the basic similarity to the "lost generation" novels of the twenties—*The Sun Also Rises, Sartoris,* but especially *The Great Gatsby*—becomes apparent. Steinbeck's Sir Henry Morgan resembles Scott Fitzgerald's Jay Gatsby far more than he does Faust, Galahad, or the historical Morgan. The parallels between the two novels are remarkable, although apparently unintentional.

Both Morgan's and Gatsby's parents were "shiftless and unsuccessful farm people" (these words are Fitzgerald's; Steinbeck is less blunt but admits that Morgan's father "was afraid to test even death"). Both invent just the sort of figure "a seventeen-year-old boy would be likely to invent" (again Fitzgerald; Morgan is only fifteen, but may have matured earlier). Both take to sea (Lake Superior—where Gatsby begins his climb—is an inland sea with a wonderfully symbolic name) and are rescued from a servile position by a wealthy and somewhat eccentric patron. Both learn wisdom by being bilked out of money. Both are characterized by "overwhelming self-absorption." Both seek great wealth after being snubbed by fashionable families. Both romanticize their backgrounds.

Both become fabulously wealthy through questionable enterprises, but find their dreams unfulfilled. Both are in love with their own vision of a woman, and both suffer when the woman fails to live up to their illusion. Here the paths separate, but they have run parallel long enough to indicate the kinship of these heroes. Gatsby dies rather than live disillusioned, but Steinbeck's hero survives to enjoy the respectable social position Gatsby found unsatisfactory. (There is a remarkable parallel between the later careers of the two authors and their respective heroes.)

No ending but Fitzgerald's would have been consistent with his melancholy concept of a decadent time; and, if Steinbeck had had the same tragic vision, disillusionment would have also hastened the death of his hero. Steinbeck, however, has always been committed to the idea, emphasized in *The Grapes of Wrath* and *The Wayward Bus,* that people must keep moving and not surrender to despair. The difference between the fate of the two heroes symbolizes not only that between the two authors' attitudes but between the group too young to have actually belonged to the "lost generation" and its predecessors who had personally felt the collapse of a world built on slogans. While Fitzgerald mourned the death of a dream, Steinbeck explored the possibility of reconciling one's self to life without illusions. Through his portrayal of Morgan, he fumbles towards a solution.

The characteristic responsible for Morgan's early ambitious drive is his single-mindedness; having settled upon a dream, he feels—like Gatsby—that he must remain faithful to it. As he tells his disappointed patron, "nothing may be allowed to interfere." In order to retain this single-mindedness one must, however, as Merlin explains, remain childlike. "You are a little boy," the old man tells Morgan when the boy explains his dream,

> "You want the moon to drink from as a golden cup; and so, it is very likely that you will become a great man—if only you remain a little child. All the world's great have been little boys who wanted the moon; running and climbing, they sometimes caught a firefly. But if one grows to a man's mind, that mind must see that it cannot have the moon and would not want it if it could—and so, it catches no fireflies."

It is sometimes assumed that this often-quoted passage expresses a sentimentalized concept of childhood as a time of joy, but when we make such an assumption we forget that the Biblical and Wordsworthian injunctions about the relationship of childhood and manhood which Steinbeck echoes here are not that children are happy and men not, but that the world seems simple to children and complex to adults. Merlin makes the distinction clear when he observes to Morgan's father:

"So . . . he has come to be the great man he thought he wanted to be. If this is true, then he is not a man. He is still a little boy and wants the moon. I suppose he is rather unhappy about it. Those who say children are happy forget their childhood."

Merlin's observation is not to be taken lightly as an indication of Steinbeck's views. It continues to occur in the author's works as late as *Sweet Thursday;* and it is reinforced by a statement of the famous diarist John Evelyn, who, in an unlikely conversation with King Charles II in *Cup of Gold,* explains that "folly and distorted vision are the foundations of greatness." Certainly this analysis fits Gatsby, Faulkner's Bayard Sartoris, and other "lost generation" heroes as long as they retain their illusions. These men, however, to use Steinbeck's Merlin's term, "stave off manhood" by destroying themselves rather than surrendering their illusions. Morgan, on the other hand, like Nick Carraway, comes to want "no more riotous excursions." Just as Nick wishes "the world . . . at a sort of moral attention forever," Morgan, after he returns from Panama, wants to "live in an atmosphere of sure things." He has lost the childlike self-assurance that is the product of single-mindedness.

This loss occurs during his interview with "La Santa Roja" after the sack of Panama; two things mark Morgan's emergence into disenchanted manhood. The first is his being forced to realize for the first time that there is a difference between his illusions and reality. When a woman calls upon him and announces that she has been "called La Santa Roja by certain young idiots," he is taken aback:

He had prepared a picture in his mind, a picture of a young girl with blue, seraphic eyes that would fall before the steady

stare of a mouse. . . . This woman's face was sharp, almost
hawk-like. She was beautiful, truly, but hers was the harsh,
dangerous beauty of lightning. . . . He was not prepared for
this change of idea. He was staggered at such a revolt against
his preconceptions.

His first disillusionment leads to his second. Throughout the
story it has been emphasized that Morgan feels that he is
"different" from other men. When one of his lieutenants compares Morgan's feelings to those of his troops, Morgan cannot
accept the comparison because "it was monstrous to think that
these men could feel as he did." His buccaneering successes
bolster his egotistical concept of his superiority. His fair captive, however, has another shock for him. When, despite his
surprise at her appearance, he makes an impassioned plea
for her to abandon her husband for him, she reacts with
amusement. He is stunned when she says,

> "I have heard your words so often and so often in Paris and
> Cordova. I am tired of these words that never change. Is there
> some book with which aspiring lovers instruct themselves?
> . . . I thought richly of you once; you grew to be a brazen
> figure of the night. And now—I find you a babbler, a speaker
> of sweet, considered words, and rather clumsy about it."

Morgan can never recapture the illusion of uniqueness; he
has been made to reach manhood—just as Merlin explains
most men are—by ridicule.

Most men would have been crushed by the damsel's contempt, but not Morgan. His future course is implied by his
reaction to the literal "cup of gold" that is the grail symbol in
the book. Steinbeck describes this object, which Morgan
dallies with after his deflating interview with La Santa Roja:
"around its outer edge four grotesque lambs chased each
other, and inside, on the bottom, a naked girl lifted her arms
in sensual ecstasy." It would be difficult not to see some kind
of innocence-knowledge imagery here, and it appears that
the lamb is employed—as Blake uses it—as a universal symbol
of childhood. The grotesqueness of the lambs symbolizes the
"distorted vision" of the great. The lambs circle the outside
of the cup, since the single-minded child sees only externals;

the carnal vision is reserved for the man who peers inside the cup and sees the world beneath the golden surface. Sensual abandonment is offered as a recompense for the man frustrated by the loss of childlike innocence and purity.

Morgan, however, rejects the cup altogether. If he is not to enjoy his own distorted vision of unique greatness, neither will he sink to the bottom and cavort with the common herd. What alternative remains? Significantly he tosses the cup into a pile of diamonds where it becomes not a symbol of childhood and manhood, but simply a token of wealth. He is prepared to compromise with the worldly concept of greatness and seek not to fulfill his own dream but to make himself very wealthy. With his gesture, he parts company with Gatsby, to whom wealth had been only a means to an end; from now on to Morgan, it is an end in itself. If La Santa Roja has surprised him, he can also surprise her. When her wealthy husband sends an envoy to ransom her, Morgan demands a fabulous amount. The staggered messenger supposes Morgan must want the woman. "No," he is told, "I want the money." When the woman learns of this transaction, she agrees to return to her dull husband. "You have pricked the dream on which my heavy spirit floated," she tells Morgan.

They have destroyed each other's illusions. That Morgan has made the choice the world deems proper is indicated when the husband's messenger is "relieved" that Morgan wants money and not the woman, because "he had been prepared to think this great man a great idiot." Later Morgan himself indicates his compliance with worldly standards when he tells the woman that he is "sick with a disease called mediocrity." Still later he tells two old piratical cohorts whom he sentences to death that "Civilization will split up a character, and he who refuses to split goes under." Gatsby goes under; Morgan splits.

Cup of Gold clearly asserts that there is no place for the swashbuckling hero in the modern world. Steinbeck feels that civilization destroys childlike innocence, so that no ambitious man can survive in society without succumbing to the mediocrity entailed in love of money. I think it is a mistake to read *Cup of Gold*, as Maxwell Geismar suggests in *Writers in Crisis*, as "advocating the free life of adventure." The novel is written in the spirit of the "debunking" biographies popular in the twenties. When Morgan announces cynically, "Hereafter I shall be gallant for two reasons only—money and advancement," he acknowledges his compromise with the realities of a commercial civilization in a way that remarkably foreshadows the behavior of the Lucky Jims of later years.

It is important, particularly in view of the ideas Steinbeck advances in later novels like *The Grapes of Wrath*, to realize that his first work is not an exercise in hero-worship but an argument that the man who expects to achieve material security must forsake illusions of unique personal greatness. The novel is not, however, a cynical recommendation to forget the dream and pursue the dollar; for Steinbeck does not advocate following Morgan's pattern. What he actually advocates is obscured by the somewhat murky symbolism of the final scene of the novel, which makes two points: first, that legend outlives truth and that what will be remembered about Morgan and La Santa Roja is not their compromise with mediocrity, but the glamorous rumors that they cultivated, for it is emphasized that when Morgan ceases to be a hero in his own eyes, he becomes more than ever a hero in the public's.

The second is that while only darkness awaits Morgan, Merlin is "herding dreams in Avalon." It is Merlin not Morgan who triumphs in the long run—Merlin who has retreated from society rather than obey his girl's injunction "to make a success of himself." Merlin contradicts Morgan's observation that he who does not split before the impact of civilization goes under. The artist (Merlin makes songs) survives if he withdraws; and it is upon the artist, of course, that the survival of the legends of Morgan and La Santa Roja will depend.

Despite the superficial pirate story, *Cup of Gold* really contrasts, therefore, the man who pursues the grail of power and finds he must compromise with society or be destroyed and the man who pursues the grail of art and transcends society. Although the book is not constructed in a manner to make this point satisfactorily, it is actually Steinbeck's first—but not his last—defense of the superiority of the artistic calling. One wonders to what extent the novel may have been inspired by a desire to answer the girl in New York who told Steinbeck that he should go into advertising before trying to make his living by creative writing.

CHAPTER 3

Resurveying the Pastures of Heaven

THE REPORT is that Pascal Covici, the editor-publisher with whom Steinbeck is particularly identified, first became interested in the writer who was to become his major literary property when induced by Chicago's astute bookman, Ben Abramson, to read *The Pastures of Heaven*. This story one can believe because it is hard to see how any sensitive reader could resist the formal mastery and emotional impact of Steinbeck's second novel. It is an ironic comment on the very obtuseness Steinbeck castigates through this novel that it still does not occupy the high place it deserves, although famous critic Maxwell Geismar in *Writers in Crisis* calls it the author's finest work.

Yet even critics like Geismar have failed to give this novel its due. Although it has been generally recognized that the ten seemingly independent stories comprising the work are too thematically interrelated for the book to be regarded merely as a collection of short stories, the over-all design of the novel has not been perceived. Geismar maintains, for example, that Steinbeck leaves the nature of the "curse" which the stories concern "a haunting question." Peter Lisca in *The Wide World of John Steinbeck* repeats a criticism that has been heard and accepted since the novel first appeared when he says that "there is no reason why one story must precede or follow another." I believe, however, that it can be demonstrated that Steinbeck does identify the "curse" that hangs over the valley and that there is a reason that governs the order in which the stories appear.

The book is held together in the first place, of course, not even so much by the common setting of the stories as by the consistently ironic tone of the narrative. That the name of the lovely valley, "The Pastures of Heaven," is ironic is stressed both by a prologue and an epilogue that frame the ten short tales about its inhabitants. From the prologue we learn that the valley was named for the impression its unspoiled beauty made on a Spanish corporal who was returning to captivity some Indians who had abandoned Christianity and returned to their carefree, primitive life. We learn also that his hopes of spending his last days contentedly in this valley went unrealized since he had to spend them instead locked in a barn where he wasted away with a pox presented him by an Indian woman.

The epilogue is even more disillusioning. Some tourists look down into the valley and regret that theirs cannot be the tranquil life it promises. Even the bus driver says as the group drives away, "I guess it sounds kind of funny to you folks, but I always like to look down there and think how quiet and easy a man could live on a little place." The reader by this time knows, however, that appearances are deceiving and that the inviting valley offers, in words Matthew Arnold had written sixty years earlier of another pleasing prospect, Dover Beach:

> . . . neither joy, nor love, nor light,
> Nor certitude, nor peace, nor help for pain. . . .

The Pastures of Heaven shelters not these things, but the Munroe family.

The Munroes provide the physical connecting link between the stories; but the novel is not so much about them—they are minor characters in all but the first episode—as about their effect upon others. Peter Lisca correctly emphasizes the importance of this family, but does not explain fully why its actions produce the results they do. He appears overimpressed with a letter Steinbeck wrote his agents discussing a family that disrupted the harmony of a valley community without ever actually committing a malicious or dishonorable act. As often, Steinbeck changed these characters to suit his purposes when fictionalizing them; the Munroes are not so innocent as those he mentions in the letter. Because the author does not, however, editorialize about them, his treatment of them in the first chapter of the book may mislead the reader.

After describing the misfortunes that have befallen the previous occupants of the house the Munroes buy, Steinbeck explains that the Munroes themselves have been the victims of frequent misfortune. The father had "engaged in many enterprises and every one had failed, not through any short-comings on Bert's part, but through mishaps, which, if taken alone, were accidents." Bert, Steinbeck continues, sees all the accidents as "the acts of a Fate malignant to his success." When Bert explains to the valley storekeeper that he hopes his curse and the one on the house have canceled each other out, the other speculates that instead maybe Bert's curse and the farm's "has mated and gone into a gopher hole like a pair of rattlesnakes," so that "there'll be a lot of baby curses crawling around the Pastures."

As indeed there are. These baby curses are the concern of individual chapters of the book. We must recall, however, that it is Bert and not Steinbeck who sees himself as haunted by a malignant fate. It is hardly likely that as skeptical a writer as Steinbeck would take seriously the notion of a "curse." Careful examination of the story shows, furthermore, that Steinbeck has provided in each a clue to a natural explanation of the Munroes' "curse"; and the novel excoriates their complacency in the face of this "natural curse" upon them.

We first learn that, before coming to the Valley, Bert Munroe had considered himself cursed because, for example, he lost a fortune when the first World War ended sooner than he expected and the price of beans dropped below what he had contracted to pay for thousands of acres of them. After moving to the Pastures, the Munroes' actions produce the following results:

(1) The false picture of affluence that "Shark" Wicks has fostered is destroyed by a chain of events growing out of Munroe's seventeen-year-old son's assumption that Wicks' beautiful but stupid daughter's response to an invitation to dance "hinted at other things which moved and excited even the cynical Jimmie."

(2) The retarded Tularecito is sent to an asylum after attacking Bert Munroe for filling in a hole that Tularecito

had been digging but that Munroe jumped to the conclusion his younger son, Manny, was digging to pester him.

(3) Mrs. Van Deventer disposes of her demented daughter as a result of troubles brought on by Bert Munroe's first assuming that he must visit the family uninvited and then making a thoughtless promise to help the daughter escape confinement.

(4) Mrs. Munroe drives Junius Maltby and his young son back to the city by forcing new clothes upon the boy that make the pair realize for the first time how impoverished they appear in the eyes of society.

(5) Munroe breaks up the Lopez' sisters "restaurant" because he thinks it a "good joke" to insinuate to a fiercely jealous woman that her husband is running off with one of the jolly sisters.

(6) Molly Morgan, the well-liked schoolteacher, feels obliged to leave the valley she loves when she hears Munroe joking crudely about a drunken hired hand whom she fears may resemble the vanished father whom she idolized.

(7) Ray Banks—a friend of the warden at San Quentin and a man of "meager imagination" who attends executions to get the satisfaction he needs, not from the events themselves but from the "throbbing nerves" of the other men attending—is deprived of this satisfaction when Munroe, begging off from an invitation he angled for but really didn't want, tells Banks that if he "had any imagination," he "wouldn't go up to see some poor devil get killed."

(8) Pat Humbert's hope of escaping the blighting burden of the past is inspired when he overhears Mae Munroe, Bert's marriageable daughter, express a passing interest in his house; he is crushed when he learns she is marrying another.

(9) John Whiteside's hope of continuing a "dynasty" of rural patriarchs is blasted when Mae Munroe marries his son and insists on moving to town and even his mansion is destroyed by a brush fire started at an inopportune time at Bert Munroe's insistence.

Studying this list, one finds something at work besides an unexplained "curse." In each episode a Munroe wreaks havoc by misjudging some aspect of a situation or by thoughtlessly saying or doing the wrong thing—the thing that will destroy the world another person has either carefully constructed for himself or come painfully to accept. At one point Steinbeck even has Mrs. Munroe unintentionally explain just what is wrong with the family: in the poignant narrative of the disillusioning of Junius Maltby (a story Steinbeck later published separately under the significant title "Nothing So Monstrous"), she, meaning only to be "nice" and "kind," says: "I think [Maltby's boy's] health is more important than his feelings." It is precisely other people's "feelings" to which the Munroes are insensitive; and, since they are callous, it never occurs to them that other people could feel differently from them—that they could be wrong about something.

Many years later in *Burning Bright,* Steinbeck was to say of a character that must be eliminated if others are to survive, "Victor's unfortunate choice it was always to mis-see, to mis-hear, to misjudge." He states specifically here what he implies through every episode in *The Pastures of Heaven;* for what is said of Victor is true of the Munroes—and of nearly all the "villainous" characters in Steinbeck's work.

Steinbeck even carefully plants a final clue to his thesis in the epilogue. A prosperous man talking about the stone keel of the Carmel Mission explains that the construction is for protection against earthquakes, but adds, "It wouldn't work." A young priest answers, "But it has worked. There have been earthquakes, and the mission still stands; built of mud and it still stands." The Munroes, like the prosperous tourist, know "what will work and what won't"; and, like him, they are wrong, because they have not bothered to discover the truth about what they are talking about. Because they are self-righteous in their wrongness, they are culpable of destroying the happiness of those they come in contact with—culpable not in the insensitive eyes of the law, but in the sensitive eyes of the compassionate artist.

The novel is thus more specifically and bitterly satirical than it is usually credited with being; perhaps the author concealed his satire too well, however, for even the perception that each episode attests to the same general failing of the Munroes does not make one fully aware of the involved structure of the novel. Specifically, the Munroes not only are at fault in each episode, but each error is graver than the preceding one.

The effect of the incidents is cumulative because the seriousness of the Munroes' offenses against the thing Steinbeck
values most highly, human dignity, can be observed to increase with each successive story. The order of the stories is
partly chronological, in that each ends at a later time than
the preceding one, but the narratives overlap; chronology is
employed only to accentuate the increasingly devastating
effect of the Munroes upon the valley. Like a skillful attorney,
Steinbeck marshals the evidence for his indictment in the
order of its seriousness and reserves the most damning exhibit
for the climax of his argument.

The Munroes' first offense against "Shark" Wicks is obviously slight and perhaps the family has done good by destroying
an illusion that has limited the effectiveness of a man and
kept his wife and daughter uncomfortable and unhappy. The
insensitive do have the advantage of failing to sentimentalize
the absurd so that their heavy touch may give a desirable
final push to tottering structures; and the reader is likely to
feel that the Munroes in this situation are on the side of progress. It is also sadly apparent in the second story that, although
Tularecito's confinement is in some ways regrettable, it is almost as inevitable and socially desirable as Benjy Compson's
in Faulkner's *The Sound and the Fury*. If Munroe had not
ended the idyll, it is very likely that the gnome-boy would
have had to be destroyed like Lennie in Steinbeck's *Of Mice
and Men*. In the story of Helen Van Deventer, Bert Munroe also does little but thoughtlessly hasten the inevitable; this time,
however, he goes out looking for trouble instead of waiting for
it to come to him.

The most ambiguous of the stories is that of Junius Maltby.
The Munroes, after all, were trying to do the "decent thing"
by clothing the needy. Although Steinbeck presents Maltby
and his son in a most favorable light, "public opinion" would
be likely to be with the Munroes. Yet here they definitely go
out of their way to destroy unthinkingly other people's illusions; they are revealing more and more the arrogance that
accompanies their ignorance. In the story of the Lopez sisters,
the case against the Munroes unmistakably intensifies. Although the sisters ply a scandalous trade, so that some will
view the Munroes as the agents of communal virtue, most

people will find the sisters inoffensive. Munroe, furthermore, destroys their happiness not as an agent of outraged morality or even decency, but simply because he thinks of "a good joke."

The scales definitely tip now against the Munroes. In the story of Molly Morgan, crude humor becomes a cruel weapon as Munroe's bragging destroys the happiness not of women of equivocal virtue but of an innocent, sensitive girl who is an unqualified asset to the community that loves her. In the story of Ray Banks, Munroe wantonly and quite deliberately sets out to destroy another man's illusions in order to protect his own. The tempo seems to diminish in the penultimate story since Mae Munroe is innocent of any direct offense against Pat Humbert. It is he who eavesdrops, who misinterprets her remarks, and who enthusiastically sets about destroying the world to which he has acclimated himself in pursuit of an idle dream.

In nearly all of his novels, especially in *The Grapes of Wrath,* Steinbeck stresses the evolutionary idea that man must adapt to changing conditions. Among the worst offenses he feels one man can commit against another is that of inhibiting the process of adaptation or of causing another to revert to a former state in self-defense. Such a reversion is precipitated by Mae Munroe's idle remark in Pat Humbert; and Steinbeck's point may well be that a thoughtless affront to human dignity—just a bit of girlish gossip—is even more serious than an intentional one since it permits the victim no redress.

The last of the tales is the most profound; since John Whiteside has made both the greatest contribution to the community and has dreamed its greatest dreams, the shattering of his real and ideal worlds would be the valley's greatest tragedy. Steinbeck writes in this chapter about more than Whitesides and Munroes; he writes a short allegory on the tragic theme of the destruction of the dream of founding a dynasty, suggesting in fifty pages the heart of the matter in such literary monuments as Thomas Mann's *Buddenbrooks* and Faulkner's *Absalom, Absalom!* It is especially interesting to compare Steinbeck's story with Faulkner's much more complex novel since both end with the burning of a great house that symbolizes the frustrated dream. The comparison with Faulkner allows us to see also that, though the parallel is far from complete, the

Munroes serve the microcosm of the Pastures of Heaven in the same way that the Snopeses serve the differently structured one of Yoknapatawpha County, Mississippi.

Since the Munroes are the agents of so much mischief, we need finally to look carefully at them to see just why Steinbeck attacks them unsparingly. Their outstanding characteristic is not even their thoughtlessness, but their mediocrity. In character sketches in the opening chapter, Steinbeck hammers home their utter lack of distinction and their yearning for the most trivial kind of security. Bert, we are told, "by stroke after stroke of genius" made his home "look like a hundred thousand other country houses in the West." Of Mrs. Munroe it is said only that once she was satisfied with the placement of a piece of furniture, "that piece was fixed forever, only to be moved for cleaning." Her daughter Mae's diary "concealed from prying eyes a completely uninteresting record of dances, of parties, of recipes for candy and of mild preferences for certain boys." Jimmie cherishes a dream of giving his life over to science, but "by science Jimmie meant radios, archeology, and airplanes." The youngest son, as a result of his parents' using the threat of an operation to remove his adenoids as a deterrent to bad behavior, is hysterical and "subnormal, his brain development arrested by his adenoidal condition."

Except for the parents' barbarously thoughtless treatment of the younger son, they are not conventionally wicked; they lack even the monomaniacal sense of self-importance of Captain Ahab or Faulkner's Snopeses. They are simply mediocrities; and, from this novel, we learn just how much Steinbeck hates the middle-class respectability for which the Munroes yearn. It is not against the wealthy and powerful that Steinbeck lashes out—even in *The Grapes of Wrath*—so much as against the man who not only is content with the *status quo* and hence a mediocrity but is also willing to destroy others to preserve it and is, therefore, a vicious mediocrity. Steinbeck considers as worst of all those whom Thoreau described as leading "lives of quiet desperation"; for they, since they know neither what they want nor what they will do to get it, are thoughtless, vicious mediocrities. In *The Pastures of Heaven*, Steinbeck outlined the strategy he employed in his warfare against the insensitive American's concept of respectability.

CHAPTER 4

Ways Out of the Wasteland

SINCE LITTLE attention had been paid Steinbeck's first two novels, his third, *To a God Unknown* (1933), did not impress the public of the early thirties as the surprise that it is to one who today reads the novels in order of publication. It marked another of the "changes of pace" for which Steinbeck was to become famous; but these changes are largely superficial, signifying not a change in the author's ideas but experiments in communicating them to a not very perceptive public.

Few have been satisfied with this third attempt; and Steinbeck never again employed the ornate, pseudo-mystical style that may represent his attempt to affiliate himself with the critically acclaimed Yeats-Eliot school of private mythologists. The book is certainly remote from the stark, simply told tales of *Of Mice and Men* and *The Grapes of Wrath* upon which Steinbeck's reputation principally depends. Actually, the novel is incomprehensible in realistic terms unless one supposes that the principal characters suffer from hallucinations. On the other hand, there are too many realistic descriptions of California landscapes and people for the book to be read as a purely symbolic fable. *To a God Unknown* is an overwrought allegory in which Steinbeck fails—as he does again in *East of Eden*—to fuse effectively realistic and symbolic elements.

What the book actually describes is the breakdown of an archetypal family. The father of the Wayne clan (the name appropriately symbolizes the decline of the family's fortunes) is somewhat vaguely represented as a Vermont farmer, but is actually a kind of totem. "I'll go right along with you," he tells his son Joseph, who is departing for fresh lands out West, "over your head, in the air . . . being up in the air like that I could see things far away." The son becomes convinced that father has come along and has settled in an oak tree, where he becomes a kind of guardian of the family fortunes to the dismay of the novel's Christianized characters.

The old man's four sons appear to symbolize man's possible conditions. Since the family has trouble getting along both in rocky Vermont and drought-stricken California, it is easy to interpret the sons and what becomes of them as an allegory of the possibilities of the survival of various types of men in the face of the vicissitudes of nature. Two of these sons, recalling the figures on the cup of gold in Steinbeck's first novel, represent the extremes of physical man; the other two, the extremes of spiritual man. In short, the group personifies body and soul, doubly dichotomized.

The youngest and shortest lived of the tribe is Benjy, a purely carnal man who represents the sensual lusts Henry Morgan saw at the bottom of the inside of the chaised cup; he does as little work as possible and spends his time drinking, singing, and seducing the women who find him irresistible. Before the novel is a third over, he is dead, stabbed in the back by a husband who has driven to town for a dehorner for a bull and "made the trip too quickly." So much for the purely sensual man; here as elsewhere Steinbeck's sympathy for the lustful irresponsible is less than some critics have supposed.

The oldest brother Thomas is a somewhat less common literary type, although he could be related to Lena in Faulkner's *Light in August*. He is the kind of purely animalistic man that Steinbeck has often been accused of writing about exclusively. He has "a strong kinship with all kinds of animals . . . but humans he neither understood nor trusted very much." He is married to Rama, a kind of earth mother, who betrays him once for symbolic purposes. He especially distrusts all rituals. On him devolves the task of holding the remnants of the family together when all are threatened by physical disaster; he is a completely reliable, unsentimental creature; but he is obviously not destined for great things.

Steinbeck is also obviously not too much interested in Thomas. Although he is treated sympathetically, he is not the

central figure in the book; he plays a role rather similar to
that of Noah Joad in *The Grapes of Wrath;* and the treatment
of both makes it clear that Steinbeck sees no hope that human
problems will be satisfactorily solved by back-to-nature types.
While Thomas survives, he is not presented in a manner that
makes purely biological survival particularly appealing. Steinbeck seems to share with Faulkner the view that man could
be more than just another animal, but that it remains to be
proved whether he can be more and endure.

Another brother, Burton, is a typical Steinbeck Christian:
he is narrow, bigoted, destructive. Representative of the
ascetic side of religion, he "kept himself from evil and he
found evil in nearly all close human contacts." He had "em-
braced his wife four times" and enjoyed gratifyingly bad
health that "proved God thought of him enough to make him
suffer." Despite all his prayers for the souls of the other members of the family, he is ultimately responsible for breaking
up the group. He moves away from the family in order to
escape its wicked ways and to enjoy the camp meetings in
Pacific Grove, where Steinbeck probably observed the type
he represents. Before leaving, however, he kills the tree that
his brother calls "the center of the land" and in which the father is believed to reside. Burton apparently survives, too; but
Steinbeck leaves the impression that, although the pious are
hard to eradicate, their state is something worse than death.

The book is principally about the fourth brother, Joseph,
who symbolizes the fecund, fructifying aspect of spiritual
man—and the difference between him and Burton is much the
same as that between the "inventor" and the "imitator" that
Emerson expounds in "The Divinity School Address." It is
Joseph who insists on leaving Vermont and satisfying his
"hunger for land" by homesteading a virgin tract in California.
Although he learns that the land he occupies in the first
decade of the twentieth century has not been cultivated previously because of a terrible drought that earlier afflicted the
region, he urges all his brothers to join him. Having been
responsible for the family's resettlement and having the
"blessing" of the father, he becomes obsessed with his role of
protector and seeks to placate any forces that might prove
inimical to the family.

Not long after he moves to California, Joseph discovers in an open glade a rock "as big as a house, mysterious and huge" which he describes as "ancient and holy" and which, according to his Indian guide, was a sacred place before the Indians' Christianization. He visits it again when he pursues this same Indian, who has killed his brother, and tells him that he will not be killed since he did what "nature demanded." Then the Indian tells him that the stream that flows from a cave in the rock reputedly comes "out of the center of the world." This information causes Joseph to realize that "his nature and the nature of the land were the same." Even before he had set out on his expedition, he had recognized that he would demand no satisfaction for his sensual brother Benjy's death; for, although others are allowed "likes and dislikes," he is "cut off" and can have "neither good luck nor bad luck" nor even "knowledge of any good or bad."

After his wife has a child, Joseph takes her to the rock, which had earlier frightened her; and there, after announcing she will climb its back and "tame" it, she slips and dies instantly. As she dies, Joseph notices that rain begins to fall, although the season is dry. This "coincidence" makes no impression on him at the time, despite his preoccupation with the effects of the drought.

Even before Joseph's wife dies, Burton has killed the tree Joseph considered sacred; and there has since been a long, serious drought. Joseph feels responsible for doing something about it, but doesn't know what. He feels that as long as the little stream "from the center of the world" flows, there is hope; but even so he prepares to move the family and remaining stock to a less afflicted region. While waiting to make this move, he and his brother Thomas make a short trip to see the ocean and meet a curious individual who is "the last man in the western world to see the sun." Each night just at sunset, he kills some little animal. Joseph becomes tremendously excited and demands that the man tell him the reason for his sacrifice, but the latter can only say: "I don't know. . . . I have made up reasons, but they aren't true." Assured by Joseph that "these were words to clothe a naked thing, and the thing is ridiculous in clothes," the man confesses, "I gave up reasons. I do this because it makes me glad. I do it because I like to." He goes on to explain:

> "Some time it will be perfect. . . . When it comes, I, myself, will go over the edge of the world with the sun. Now you know. In every man this thing is hidden. It tries to get out, but a man's fears distort it. He chokes it back. What does get out is changed—blood on the hands of status, emotion over the story of an ancient torture—the giving or drawing of blood in copulation."

The whole unlikely incident seems a disgression, but it turns out to be the climax of the story; for, after meeting this man, Joseph refuses to leave the land, which he identifies with himself, to move with the family. Instead he begins to live near the mysterious rock. Finally when the drought remains unbroken and the stream that gushes from the rock dries up, Joseph thinks of the old man and remarking, "This might be the way," sacrifices a calf. Nothing happens, and he concludes that the old man's secret "was for him" and won't work for others. As a last resort, however, he decides to climb to the top of the rock. Then

> . . . he took out his knife again and carefully, gently opened the vessels of his wrist. . . . The sky was growing grey. And time passed and Joseph grew grey too. He lay on his side with his wrist outstretched and looked down the long black mountain range of his body. Then his body grew huge and light. It arose into the sky, and out of it came the streaking rain. "I should have known," he whispered. "I am the rain. . . . I am the land . . . and I am the rain. The grass will grow out of me in a little while."

Steinbeck could hardly have intended this scene to be taken literally. He probably means to imply that Joseph makes his sacrifice not because it has some magical efficacy, but because, like the old man, he likes to do it. Since Joseph is the central character, the point of the allegory seems to be that man's highest good is found not in survival, but in being true to his own secret nature—an idea that brings to mind, not only Thoreau but also unfortunately Savonarola, Huey Long, and anyone with a "call." What the old man by the Pacific calls "hidden" may be an innate affinity with the basic rhythms of nature; but it may also be, as brother Thomas suspects, insanity. Whatever it is, the lustful man, the animalistic man, the ascetic can never know it nor surrender their own personalities in order to be absorbed back into the wholeness of nature, "the unknown god," presumably what Emerson would have called "the oversoul." The complex allegory proves finally to be a vivid illustration of the hardly original thesis that man and nature are essentially one and that one fulfills one's self by a reunion with nature even at the cost of self-destruction.

Steinbeck's solution to the problem of the wasteland is then to re-establish this basic unity, physically, as Joseph does when he has intercourse with his brother's wife Rama, dispassionately and ritualistically, not from hunger but need. That Steinbeck had such an allegory in mind and did not mean to indicate that Joseph felt problems would work themselves out is evident from Joseph's angry reply to a priest who has told him that "the land does not die": "How do you know? The deserts were once alive. Because a man is sick often, and each time gets well, is that proof that he will never die?"

One's reaction to the story depends upon one's interpretation of the behavior of the central character; if one finds Joseph Wayne more psychopathic than altruistic (and what educators would call "a slow learner" in the bargain), one is likely to have little patience with the rest of the book. Steinbeck may, of course, have intended Joseph to be viewed as insane; one of the priest's speeches—"Thank God this man has no message. Thank God he has no will to be remembered, to be believed in . . . else there might be a new Christ here in the West"—suggests that the whole novel may be intended to satirize the Messianic complex. If so, the satire got lost in pseudo-mysticism; the story would have had more human implications if Joseph, like Mac in *In Dubious Battle* or Casy in *The Grapes of Wrath*, had had a message. If the point is simply that one should do what he likes, readers may find it hard to identify with a character who ends up slashing his wrists ritualistically.

CHAPTER 5

Morte d'Malory

STEINBECK'S fourth published novel is a landmark in his career because it was the first to win him both public and critical recognition. It has remained a primary exhibit of those who charge him with being preoccupied with loafers. Both approving and disapproving critics of this purported penchant have usually missed, however, the subtly ironic point of the book, whose hardihood seems proved by its having survived two successive stages of misinterpretation.

The book was first regarded—occasionally still is—as a kind of glorification of man in his least inhibited state. Certainly its initial success is attributable to its purported praise of irresponsibility. Appearing during the depths of the depression when the readers—if not the socially conscious critics— wanted to be told about people happy with even less than they had, *Tortilla Flat* provided, like Kaufman and Hart's *You Can't Take It With You,* a sought-after escape. But Steinbeck's *paisanos* are not the Vanderhofs of Broadway. Their creator did not devise them as a quaint antidote for depressionitis, and the novel does not end on a gloriously optimistic note of material renunciation. The novel's being frequently admired, almost as often decried, and occasionally banned for being a kind of Rousseauesque idyll when it is really something quite different has not, however, hindered this work that Steinbeck regarded as second-rate from becoming a minor modern classic.

A second stage of interpretation of *Tortilla Flat* began with Lewis Gannett's publication in 1943 in the introduction to the *Portable Steinbeck* of a letter Steinbeck had written to his agents in 1934. In answer to criticisms that the novel was formless, Steinbeck explained that it followed a definite pattern based on the Malory version of the Arthurian legends, and he even offered to add to the book inter-chapters like those later used in *The Grapes of Wrath* that would comment upon the moral, aesthetic, and historical significance of the incidents. These chapters were not added, but chapter titles in the manner of those of the Caxton edition of Malory's *Morte d'Arthur* were supplied.

Gannett apparently accepted the letter at face value; and, since Steinbeck himself insisted on the Arthurian parallel in the preface to the Modern Library edition of the novel, there has been an effort to read *Tortilla Flat* as an up-to-date, down-to-earth Arthurian legend. The results have been both provocative and grotesque. Peter Lisca has pointed out that there are impossible difficulties in "squaring the details given in Steinbeck's letter with the incidents and characters" of the novel and indicated his suspicion that Steinbeck "exaggerated the book's parallel to Malory in order to impress some publisher."

Lisca is right; those who seek detailed parallels between the two books are likely to be as frustrated as most grail hunters. About all Steinbeck's letter suggests is that he followed the very general plan of the formation, flowering, and destruction of King Arthur's troop; parallels to these are apparent enough in the gathering of Danny's friends in his house, their doing remarkable deeds in the neighborhood, and the dissolution of their bond following Danny's death. It takes more than such general similarities, however, to make an Arthurian legend, or else almost every television Western about the formation of a posse would qualify as a Round Table myth. There are also matters of tone to consider.

A clue to a convincing interpretation may be found in Steinbeck's one specific reference to an Arthurian parallel in his tale. He supposed that even his treatment of the search in the forest for the Sangreal was not clear enough; it certainly wasn't, because it isn't even clear which incident he refers to. Lisca supposes that it is Pilon's hunt in the woods on St. Andrew's Eve, but points out that this parallel is inaccurate since the search for the grail led to the disbandment of the Round Table. It is equally possible, however, that the search for the grail is the search for Danny that his friends make in the woods in Chapter Fifteen after Danny has run away, because it is Danny's flight and the search for him that lead directly to the dissolution of the group. Actually it doesn't matter which incident is referred to, since both illustrate the same relationship between *Tortilla Flat* and the *Morte d'Arthur*.

In the earlier St. Andrew's Eve episode, after a night's digging for "mystic treasure," Pilon and Big Joe unearth a marker of the United States Geodetic Survey. Instead of the spiritual treasure they seek, they find a mundane symbol that it would mean a year in jail to steal and sell. The satire on treasure seekers is apparent, but there is more than gentle satire here. The Geodetic Survey markers are not just any prosaic symbol; they are buried indicators in the forest of the orderly methodical civilization that is closing in on the undisciplined *paisanos*. Their quest brings them face to face not with a romantic reward but with only another evidence of the ubiquity of an incomprehensibly systematic government.

The same satirical purpose underlies the more significant search for Danny. Steinbeck describes one day's events:

> The paisanos ranged all day through the woods, calling Danny's name, looking in places they themselves might have chosen to sleep in . . . but they found no sign of Danny. . . .
>
> In the evening they went back to Danny's house and opened the door and went in. Instantly they became intense. A thief had been busy. Danny's blankets were gone. All the food was stolen. Two pots were missing.

While the knights were out seeking the grail, someone had broken in and stolen their necessities. Such an experience would not entice one a-grailing. The irony of leaving the home front undefended while roaming about on a chivalrous quest is strengthened when it becomes apparent that the thief is Danny himself, who finally when he steals Pilon's shoes commits "a crime against friendship" (like Launcelot's seduction of Guenevere) that is the symbol of the imminent dissolution of the bond.

Whichever incident one interprets as the Grail incident, it is evident that Steinbeck is actually using the *Morte d'Arthur* satirically. Like Mark Twain, but less obviously, he is burlesquing rather than retelling chivalric legends; and *Tortilla Flat,* far from marking a break with Steinbeck's earlier works, carries on and clarifies the satirical intentions of *Cup of Gold, The Pastures of Heaven,* and perhaps even *To a God Unknown.* But just what is Steinbeck satirizing in *Tortilla Flat?* —the same respectable middle-class mediocrity that had been his target previously?

The respectable middle-class is roughly handled in *Tortilla Flat.* Steinbeck satirizes it directly: "Imagine going to a funeral without first polishing the automobile. Imagine standing at the graveside not dressed in your best dark suit." He also obliquely burlesques bourgeois values by glorifying *paisano* life: "Gentlemen," a doctor says after he has visited Teresina Cortez's children, "They are living on what constitutes a slow poison, and they have from birth. Gentlemen, I tell you, I have never seen healthier children in my life." His desire to satirize pretentious middle-class mediocrities accounts for Steinbeck's exaggerated but somewhat tongue-in-cheek praise of the *paisanos* that has sometimes been taken as providing the book's principal purpose; this satire, however, is sporadic and actually incidental to the main tenor of the work.

The organized church, which had also been spoken of unkindly in *Cup of Gold* and *To a God Unknown,* is treated with little courtesy in *Tortilla Flat.* Although the scene in which a vision is accorded Pirate's dogs after he has repeated a sermon to them is sometimes cited as an example of sentimentality, it is really rather cynical to depict a pack of mongrels as the only ones in the book granted a vision. Nor could the church be particularly pleased by Steinbeck's observation: "It must be admitted with sadness that Pilon had neither the stupidity, the self-righteousness, nor the greediness for reward ever to become a saint." The references to religion are, however, also incidental; the qualifications for sainthood are discussed only to prepare for an explanation that it was "enough for Pilon to do good and be rewarded by the glow of human brotherhood accomplished."

The target of most of the satire is the very group Steinbeck has been accused of glamourizing—the indolent barbarians who hope to enjoy benefits of civilization without contributing to it. Peter Lisca points out that the *paisanos* are not the thoughtless animals some critics have assumed and explores the rationalizations they devise to justify their shortcomings; but he does not fully suggest the emptiness of their lives as Steinbeck depicts them.

The point of *Tortilla Flat* is partially that the way of life of these "bums" is in some ways superior to the average American's and that we might learn something from them; but it is also partially a warning that the simple, close-to-nature life that some men think they long for is not the answer to society's problems either. Steinbeck is here, as elsewhere, not so much exalting the "have-nots" as attacking the "haves"; there is a great difference between these two activities, although people in general and Americans in particular are prone to the fallacy of false obversion. Still the average person could hardly be expected to appreciate very much Steinbeck's ranking him even below a group of people who amounted to almost nothing.

The story of Danny is actually an extended illustration of Henry Morgan's observation in *Cup of Gold* that "civilization will split up a character, and he who refuses to split goes under." Danny is established in the preface to the book as a kind of legendary wild man. Discharged from the service, he strolls along Alvarado Street breaking windows; jailed, he names dead bedbugs for city officials. He is an epic hero—the kind of unrestrained individual that every man who has succumbed to civilization fancies he would like to be and whom the frustrated reader hopes can escape and triumph over civilization, since such escape or triumph would be vicariously his own. Like the mythical cowboy, Danny is the apotheosis of those who, Thoreau said, lead "lives of quiet desperation."

Tortilla Flat is a novel, however, not of escape, but defeat. Danny does not flee (soon enough, anyway) into the forest, but faces civilization and tries to make it come to terms with him instead of "splitting" before it. His temptation comes in the form of two small houses he inherits from his grandfather, and the end is foreshadowed on the first page where we learn that, when Danny heard about the houses, "he was a little weighed down with the responsibility of ownership." If this were escapist fiction, Danny would have either disposed of the houses immediately or miraculously parlayed them into a subdivision; instead he moves in and tries to live partly in the manner of the comfortable burgher and partly in a fashion superior to the burgher's by sharing his property with his friends and aiding those in distress. His friend Pilon's observation, however, that "the worry of property was settling on Danny's face" is followed by the significant remark: "No more in life would that face be free of care." Steinbeck implies that once one challenges civilization there is no drawing back.

For a while Danny and his entourage flourish by living in a "natural," uninhibited manner—trying, like Jesus Maria Corcoran, to relieve suffering and look at girls' legs because they like to, or expressing, like Big Joe, urges when they strike them, even if the impulse is procreative and the place the middle of a muddy street in view of a policeman.

Nature alone is not, however, enough. As Danny and his friends settle down to a routine in their home, Danny, who has never before been conscious of the clock, begins "to feel the beating of time." When he looks at his friends, he sees how "with them every day was the same," and he begins to long for the "good old days" when "the weight of property was not upon him." His friends try to help, but "it was not coddling Danny wanted, it was freedom." In the end, he surrenders to his longing and disappears into the woods. But now he finds the wild life difficult and exhausting. Finally he betrays his friends by selling his house; when his friends repossess it by trickery, he is obliged to return, beaten and apathetic. To rouse him, his friends throw a party that becomes a legend in the region.

At the height of this bacchanale, Danny grows "huge and terrible" and, grabbing a table-leg, challenges all present. When none will fight, he shouts, "Then I will go out to The One who can fight. I will find The Enemy who is worthy of Danny!" He stalks out. Then his friends

> . . . heard his roaring challenge. . . . And then, behind the house, in the gulch, they heard an answering challenge so fearful and so chill that their spines wilted like nasturtium stems under frost. . . . They heard Danny charge to the fray. They heard his last shrill cry of defiance, and then a thump. And then silence.

Steinbeck never specified who the fearsome "Opponent" is. Each reader may interpret the phrase for himself as referring to God, Fate, some cycle of nature, or whatever he envisions as imposing limits upon man and obliging him to conform to some system rather than live a law unto himself. Maxwell Geismar interprets the phrase in what may be the most satisfactory way as referring to "the spectre of civilization" within one's self. Danny has set himself up against this opponent—this personal Moby Dick—and has been defeated. He has refused to "split" before the demands of civilization and, as Henry Morgan prophesied, he goes under. Danny tries to play the role of a great man; but what Pablo says of Bob Smoke applies also to the leader of the band: "Whenever he tries to be a great man, something happens and everybody laughs." While everyone does not laugh at Danny, "The Opponent" does.

As a heroic tale, *Tortilla Flat* is ultimately a tragedy—another tragedy of the man who tries to attain greatness but who does not succeed—as all three of Steinbeck's preceding novels had been from at least one viewpoint. Steinbeck does not point out Danny's tragic flaw specifically, but he gives an inkling of it by ironically having Danny observe of another man, a petty servant of civilization, the dog-catcher: "It is not so easy to catch dogs when it is your business to catch dogs." It is easy to dream of freedom, but not to be a free agent. Danny does not have the resources that would enable him either to adjust to a new life or to revert to an old one.

The point then in relationship to the *Morte d'Arthur* is that there is no room in the civilized world for the Arthurian hero, if indeed there was ever a place for him in any world. Steinbeck and Malory write from different points of view. What little we know about Malory—or about the life of the man we suppose to be the author of the nostalgic Arthurian romances—suggests that he was a cultural reactionary, who longed, like Edwin Arlington Robinson's Miniver Cheevy, for a lost world. He collected the legends of that epoch and reshaped them into his own idealized concept of the past. The literary men of our era who most nearly resemble Malory are not writers like Steinbeck, but the Southern Agrarians, who have attempted to make of Calhoun and the ante-bellum

South what Malory made of Arthur and his imaginary England. As James C. Kehl has pointed out in a perceptive essay "Defender of the Faith" (*South Atlantic Quarterly,* Spring, 1960), the fictional character of our era who most resembles Malory's Arthur is not Steinbeck's Danny but Daddy Warbucks of the Little Orphan Annie comic strip.

Danny does not resemble Malory's Arthur, but the historical Malory. The parallel between this knight—the leader of a band of outlaws who was guilty of assault, robbery, rape, and attempted murder—and Danny is suggested by the report that on May 25, 1450, Malory broke into a Hugh Smyth's house and raped his wife Joan and the furious wine-seller Torrelli's account of a visit from Danny:

> "My wife he insulted and me he called bad names. My baby he spanked, my dog he kicked! He stole the hammock from my porch. . . . I chased him to get my hammock back, and when I returned, he was with my wife!"

Steinbeck could certainly have sensed why the legendary Arthur must have had such an appeal to the violent knight. Lisca reports that Steinbeck describes the Arthurian legends as a key to the understanding of our subconscious attitudes; and one thing Steinbeck could have had in mind is that the uninhibited knight who collected these tales must have had a passionate longing for a world that was no more and probably never was: a world where man was a law unto himself and where all who opposed him were demons to be destroyed. He must have hated not only a civilization that put physical restraints upon him but also law and other systematic abstractions upon which the maintenance of civilized society depended.

Whoever the original Arthur was, he was probably what we today would call a hoodlum, a petty chieftain whose brazen prowess attracted admiration and who after his death became the subject of legends that glossed over his failings and endowed his violence with a spiritual significance. One who doubts that the trappings of the Grail quest are consistent with hooliganism need only observe the growing confusion of lawmen and outlaw in the legends of our own West and the fanciful titles and costumes adopted by today's street gangs.

In the preface to *Tortilla Flat*, Steinbeck says that he wishes to record the cycle of tales about Danny and his friends before they circulate too widely and are assumed to be purely legendary. This statement has usually been interpreted as meaning that he wished to shape a legend about the joys of irresponsibility; it is at least as likely, however, that what he had in mind was presenting an unvarnished picture of a pseudo-hero that might serve to discredit rather than reinforce glamorous older legends of the same species.

Danny is a pseudo-hero not just because he has limitations, but even more because he fails to recognize them. *Tortilla Flat*, drolly as it is written, is primarily a tragedy, a dark epic of the defeat of the anarchical personality. Yet in another sense, it is comic since the self-destruction of disorder is a step toward the triumph of order. The real point of the book, however, is satirical; it is a caustic criticism by a man who knows that the principle that what does not change dies applies to societies as well as individuals—a criticism of change-fearing mediocrity that pathetically deifies the uncivilized. The novel is not a sentimental valedictory for simple-minded irresponsibility but a shrewd ribbing of those who lead lives of "quiet desperation" and whose indiscriminating response to the barbaric makes them even more despicable than the untutored savage.

CHAPTER 6

Parsifal's Last Stand

STEINBECK'S interest in Arthurian legendry has been frequently commented upon; but his fifth novel, *In Dubious Battle*, seems not to have been considered as a modern gloss on a significant part of these legends. Yet, although the quaint language and chapter headings are missing, an Arthurian echo is as conspicuous here as in *Tortilla Flat* in the remarkable psychological similarity between Jim Nolan, the central character of the novel, and one of the principal knights of the Round Table, Perceval, or Parsifal as he is best known as a result of Wagner's festival opera.

Just what *In Dubious Battle* is—besides being remarkably different from Steinbeck's previous novels—has puzzled critics. Although it describes the role of Communist agitators in an agricultural strike, it is generally agreed that it is not a radical or proletarian novel. Steinbeck insisted that it was not a tract; and, when one reads it at a time removed from the tensions engendered by the events it describes, one becomes aware that it is not even primarily about a strike. Certainly it is not a "timely" novel in the sense that it deals with subjects of only transient or regional interest; nor is it a work that seeks to provide answers for the problems it poses. Steinbeck expected the novel to anger both sides in the dispute he depicted; if the disputants had read serious fiction, it unquestionably would have.

In Dubious Battle was perhaps misread because it is Steinbeck's first full-length novel in the simple, lucid, objective style that he had perfected in the short stories of *The Red Pony* cycle and that he was to use with distinction in his most significant fiction. The novel is remarkable for the utter absence of editorial comment, for Steinbeck managed a more rigidly restricted point of view than he employed in any of his other works with as much skill as Henry James did in some of his highly praised novels. The reader sees and hears only what Jim Nolan does from the moment he decides to offer his services to the Communists until his death. Though other characters are sometimes spotlighted, Jim is never off-stage.

Obviously the author wishes the reader to associate himself in some way with Jim. One might first suppose that the identification the author sought would be with the young idealist's search for a Cause. Even in the troubled thirties, however, it is doubtful if many could have identified themselves with Jim; his situation was too special. If Steinbeck had wished to make him a typically rebellious adolescent, he would have done better to picture him as oppressed by his environment and motivated by a vaguely defined desire to do good for mankind—the kind of feeling that sent young Americans like Flem Snopes's "daughter" in Faulkner's *The Mansion* to fight for Loyalist Spain or that later accounted for the perplexities of Holden Caulfield (in the fervent thirties, as in some parts of the world today, some Utopian cause would surely have caught "the catcher in the rye").

Many might have shared, of course, Jim's indignation at being unjustly jailed as a participant in a radical meeting he was not even attending; but the peculiar make-up of his family—a father who had been killed while dynamiting a slaughterhouse, a mother who wasted away after being cut off from the church that gave her life meaning, a sister who unaccountably vanished upon achieving puberty—certainly distinguishes him from the usual idealistic adolescent in rebellion against a complacent, insensitive family. Perceval in *Morte d'Arthur* also has a father slain by treachery, a morose mother, and a sister who dies and mysteriously disappears.

Jim Nolan is further isolated from most of his fellows by his freedom from social vices. He neither smokes, drinks, nor goes with girls, although he had done some of these things before he started to grow up. It is hard to account for his purity unless Steinbeck wishes to differentiate him from ordinary young men and give him a special allegorical significance; and personal purity is, of course, the characteristic most cultivated by the Knights of the Round Table. According to one part of Malory's book, only Galahad is allowed to see the Grail because he has been a "clean maiden" and Wagner's Parsifal alone can set matters aright because he is a "guileless fool." Steinbeck's Jim is hardly credible as a contemporary character, but he serves well as a modern exemplar of the chivalric ideals of adventurousness (he longs for action and is finally killed by his impetuousness), selflessness, and chastity. The realistic language and setting have prevented readers from observing that the novel may be profitably read as an ironic and pessimistic allegory of the fate of the chivalric spirit in the modern world.

Certainly Steinbeck shows little optimism in his portrayal of the central figure. Jim's nature is somewhat obscured through the first two-thirds of the book because he is serving his "squireship" to a battle-tested knight, Mac, upon whom emphasis somewhat misleadingly falls, and also because, as a result of the limited viewpoint Steinbeck uses, we do not learn Jim's thoughts or see him except through the eyes of those who are exploiting him. We learn only that he is attached to the Party as men became attached to the Round Table because the group seemed to be "working towards something."

We learn more about him late in the book when he says that "it seems good" to have a wound in his shoulder, and Dr. Burton replies, "I thought it might be something like that." When Jim asks what, Burton continues, "I mean you've got something in your eyes, Jim, something religious. I've seen it in you boys before." Jim flares up and denies that he is religious, but he has missed the doctor's point. The matter comes up again. When Jim tells the doctor that since he has begun working for the Cause, he's not "lonely any more," the doctor replies, "Pure religious ecstasy. . . . Partakers of the blood of the lamb." Jim angrily replies, "This is men, not God," but the doctor asks only, "Well, can't a group of men be God, Jim?" Jim, like Hazel in *Cannery Row*, is shocked and troubled by such unprecedented speculations.

That Jim is, however, a young man with something analogous to a religious "call" becomes apparent when the sight of Mac beating up a high school boy who has been sniping at the strikers suddenly illuminates him. In the first chapter, a Communist organizer has told Jim that he will lose his hatred and that he will be surprised when he stops hating people. What he meant suddenly strikes Jim, who explains that seeing the boy beaten led him to recognize that "sympathy is as bad as fear." The beating was like "a doctor's work," just an "operation."

Following this relevation, Jim announces that he is taking command. "I wanted to be used," he tells Mac; "Now I'll use you. . . . I tell you, I feel there's a strength in me." Mention of his purity returns like a Wagnerian *leitmotif*. He is taking over, he explains, because "I'm stronger than anything in the world because I'm going in a straight line. You and all the rest have to think of women and tobacco and liquor and keeping warm and fed." He exercises command effectively. When at the climactic moment in the narrative, after one strike leader by beating another has rekindled the enthusiasm of the nervous and apathetic strikers, it is Jim who, pointing his clasped hands down the road, gives the signal for the attack upon the barricades that turns the tide in favor of the strikers.

Jim's triumph is, however, short-lived; although his leadership is recognized and he is chosen to talk the men into fighting rather than running, he becomes carried away with his enthusiasm and allows himself to be lured into the hands of the enemy and killed. (His utility does not end with his death, however, since Mac drags his body back to incite the men into continuing the fight.) The guileless fool has been destroyed; to emphasize that the book is about Jim, not the strike, the author ends it here with the outcome of the strike uncertain. Nor does he leave its outcome up to the reader as he will the fate of the Joads in *The Grapes of Wrath;* what happens no longer really matters. The author's point is made; the virtuous knight-errant has been destroyed by a blast in the dark.

The book could, of course, be merely an ironic commentary on the fate of the zealot in any situation, but that would leave too many things unexplained. Looking back from the conclusion, one can appreciate the double-edged sword of satire Steinbeck swings.[1] It is apparent all the way through the book that Steinbeck is out of sympathy with the entrenched and inflexible capitalists represented by the Torgas Valley apple growers. It could be argued, in fact, that, as a case study, the novel is unbalanced since the growers' side is given only briefly; but Steinbeck undoubtedly felt that both their case and the radical case against them were sufficiently well publicized. What needed to be made clear to an audience that tended to see radicals as either all good or all bad was just what attracted men to an organization like the Communist Party and what made this attraction disastrous.

Before examining the treatment of the Communists, however, we should observe that Steinbeck is really condemning the society in power most harshly not for opposing the strikers, but for mishandling young men like Jim Nolan. Whatever else he might have been, Jim was an earnest and energetic young man, capable of intense dedication to whatever cause he served; it is an indictment of a self-satisfied society that it failed to provide constructive channels for the employment of this energy and sense of dedication. With Swiftian bitterness, Steinbeck satirizes a society that destroys rather than cherishes the chivalric spirit.

Since the established culture fails to utilize the talents of its potential knights-errant, they fall into the hands of extremists. Thus far the novel might be considered the work of an idealistic, radical sympathizer, but such a writer would stress the nobility of working for a Cause. If Steinbeck lashes reactionaries, he does not spare the radicals.

The case against the Communists is summed up in the portrayal of Mac, who, it becomes clear as the story progresses, is more interested in power than people. It is never really clear why he joined the Communists; he explains that he was beaten by ex-soldiers for making a speech saying that people were starving, but he does not describe the circumstances in which the speech was made. In view of his subsequent behavior, one suspects he may have been more interested in fomenting trouble than feeding folks. Indeed one of the clearest revelations of his character comes when he says to Jim, "I took a leave and went into the woods in Canada. Say, in a couple of days, I came running out of there. I wanted trouble, I was hungry for a mess." Whatever Mac may be, he is no Thoreau.

As their association develops, Jim becomes increasingly aware that Mac is contemptuous of people. His attitude manifests itself during his description of his beating by the soldiers, when he speaks of the "nice" soldiers he knew in France as "good, honest, stupid cattle." His addiction to blood is stressed. He tells Jim, "There's nothing like a fight to cement the men together." Later when matters get desperate, he comments that what the strikers need is blood, because "a mob's got to kill something."

What really disconcerts Jim, however, is his discovery that Mac's taste for blood is accompanied by a lack of respect for individual human dignity. "Suppose they do kill some of our men?" he asks, when Jim protests that the armed men may attack the strikers, "for every man they kill ten new ones come over to us." Dakin, a strike leader, has correctly labeled Mac "a cold-blooded bastard"; he earned the epithet earlier when he told Jim, "We can't waste time liking people" and on another occasion, "I can't take time to think about the feelings of one man." He thinks of all people, even the dead, only in terms of how they can be used to advance the Cause. It is clear that to Steinbeck, Mac is like one of those military strategists or bureaucrats who think of people only as "personnel."

Near the end of the book, Jim questions even Mac's loyalty to the Cause. "Sometimes," he says, "I get the feeling you're not protecting me for the Party, but for yourself." Mac clearly likes to manipulate men. When Jim asks, after first meeting Mac, whether Mac is the boss of a group of agitators, the other replies, "I tell 'em what to do, but they don't have to do it. I can't issue any orders. The only orders that really stick are the ones that come down after a vote." This sounds like selfless discipline until we later hear Mac tell one of the strike leaders, "If you want 'em to vote for something, you say 'do you want to do it?' and if you want to vote down somethin', just say 'you don't want to do this, do you?' and they'll vote no." Mac even once in a moment of candor suggests his true relation to the Party. "Everybody hates us," he says; "our own side and the enemy. If we won Jim, if we put it over, our own side would kill us. I wonder why we do it?"

Mac does it because he has a lust for power. Steinbeck had

had the opportunity to witness the Communist purges of the thirties (repeated during the struggle for power after the death of Stalin). He views the subordination of the individual to a Cause as an affront to human dignity, because he perceives that, since a "cause" is an abstraction after all, what one seeks in its name is only what one wants for one's self. Mac's self-seeking is apparent from the contrast between his early explanation that he is helping the strikers because he feels the way men do for their friends "about all the workin' stiffs in the country" and his later explanation that "this whole strike's worth it if London [one of the strike leaders] comes over [to the Party]."

The organizers are just as much exploiters as the growers. The case against them is summarized in the savagely ironic symbol of Jim's faceless body at the end of the book. Mac brings the body back to a meeting of the strikers and places a lantern "carefully on the floor, so that its light [falls] on the head." This gesture makes explicit Steinbeck's objection to the exploiters of human dignity: seeking to serve those who place something above a man, Jim ends up not only dead, but faceless.

Steinbeck has a further criticism of the Communists. In a conversation, Doctor Burton tells Jim, "You can only build a violent thing with violence." Since Burton, a medical doctor who voluntarily assists the strikers, is the most admirable character in this novel, or in any of Steinbeck's up to this point, his words merit special consideration. Although Steinbeck makes no direct acknowledgment of any influence of Thoreau or Gandhi upon his thinking, he shared their concepts of individual dignity; it is not, therefore, out of the question to look for their idea of passive resistance in his work. The agitators are not only prone to violence, however, but actually hostile to thinking their position through. After the conversation mentioned earlier about the nature of religion, Jim loses his temper and Burton says simply, "All of you people get angry when you're asked a question." People who might effect worthwhile changes should be able to examine their motives; but the Communists in this book are as anti-intellectual as Benjy in *To a God Unknown* and Danny in *Tortilla Flat*.

The battle of the title is "dubious" not as might at first be supposed because it is in doubt which side will win the strike, but because there is doubt about the merits of both sides. Much later in *A Russian Journal,* Steinbeck speaks of "the ecclesiastical left" and "the lumpen right." *In Dubious Battle* shows both in action—between them, they destroy the spirit of chivalry. It should be observed that the attack on the radicals here is not exclusively an attack on Communism; it is an attack on one form of radicalism as a symbol of any fiercely held partisan abstraction that violates human dignity.

In Dubious Battle is not, however, merely a curse on two houses; for a third force is introduced in the novel. Doctor Burton is presented as a man willing to help the strikers, but unwilling to join the Party. Another similarity between the opposed sides is illustrated when the doctor's refusal to sign up is as incomprehensible to the Communists as his willingness to help the strikers is to the growers. Burton, however, tries to explain to Mac that he has no illusions about the Cause:

> "There've been communes before, and there will be again. But you people have an idea that if you can *establish* the thing, the job'll be done. Nothing stops, Mac. If you were able to put an idea into effect tomorrow, it would start changing right away. Establish a commune, and the same gradual flux will continue."

Mac is not interested in such theories; like his opponents, he can think only in terms of right and wrong; and, like the woman in "The White Quail," he longs to establish an unchanging garden. "Then you don't think the cause is good?" he asks. Burton tries to explain:

> "I want to see the whole picture—as nearly as I can. I don't want to put on the blinders of 'good' and 'bad,' and limit my vision. If I used the term 'good' on a thing, I'd lose my license to inspect it, because there might be bad in it. Don't you see? I want to be able to look at the whole thing."

Mac does not see. His is a partisan vision, and he cannot understand what Burton means when he says, "I don't believe in the cause, but I believe in men." Mac, as has been shown, neither believes in nor likes people. Although he is offended when Burton says of his effect upon a crowd, "No preacher ever brought people to the mourners' bench quicker . . . you'd have had them talking in tongues and holy-rolling in a minute," the doctor has correctly perceived that Mac is fundamentally ecclesiastical. The doctor is not an ecclesiast; he is a scientist. He wishes not to stir men, but study them: "It might be worthwhile to know more about group-man, to know his nature, his ends, his desires. . . . I simply want to see as much as I can, Mac, with the means I have." Mac wishes not to study but to stir men and distrusts even talk of objective, scientific study. "If he wasn't a doctor," he says of Burton, "we couldn't have 'im around. We need his skill, but his brain just gets us into a mess."

Since Burton is the first character Steinbeck has presented completely sympathetically, it is important to observe that his arguments go unanswered. Even in this objective novel, Steinbeck implies that the doctor's brain is the only thing that might actually keep people out of a mess, but that he is disregarded by the fanatics. Burton is almost the first man of pure good will to appear in a Steinbeck novel, the first to say, "I have some skill in helping men, and when I see men who need help, I just do it," the first to do it without making some kind of ritual of it. His altruism contrasts vividly with the selfishness of the conflicting groups, contrasts so vividly in fact that he is the most memorable character in the book. Perhaps Steinbeck intended him to be, but his dominance turns the novel into a kind of tract, after all.

Yet if *In Dubious Battle* is a cry in the partisan jungle for men of good will, it remains pessimistic. Especially foreboding in this novel are Burton's failure to communicate with Jim and his eventual disappearance. The latter is simply explained. Called out to help a sick man one day, he vanishes; although the mystery is never cleared up, it is implied that he has been destroyed by one of the passionate partisans. Steinbeck's grim conclusion is that the man of good will who refuses to be partisan will be destroyed by those irrationally committed to sides.

In the long run, however, Burton's frustrating relationship with Jim is even more tragic than his disappearance. Burton is the one person in the novel from whom Jim might learn how to channel his energies constructively. But when Burton advocates that Jim really learn his business—"you start your work not knowing your medium. And your ignorance trips you up every time"—Mac simply denounces his ideas with the benighted's stock phrase for the enlightened, "high-falutin'." Jim picks up the word and the attitude behind it. Later when Burton tries to tell Jim that "the other side is made of men . . . men like you" and to get him to examine his position, Jim simply replies, "You build a trap of words and then you fall into it. You can't catch me. Your words don't mean anything to me. I know what I'm doing. Argument doesn't have any effect on me."

It doesn't, and what he's doing is preparing to go faceless to his grave. It is only too true that the doctor's words don't "mean anything" to him. Immediately after this conversation, Burton disappears, his questions unanswered. The voice of reason has not cut through the fog of emotion in which "practical" men move; as Burton observes, "In all history there are no men who have come to such wild-eyed confusion and bewilderment as practical men leading men with stomachs." Steinbeck wished the reader to associate himself with Jim so that he will be shocked by the tragic waste the young man's death represents. The reader is called upon not to support but to suspect "causes."

In Dubious Battle is not so much about strikes and strikers as about the attempt of men of good will to make themselves heard in a world torn by partisan passions. Since such passions are still rampant, it remains a timely novel; it will remain timely as long as men ask, "Is it good or bad?" before they ask "What is it?" This is a pessimistic novel in that the author sees little promise of men's becoming enlightened but it is not by any means what Steinbeck has often been said to write—a fatalistic or naturalistic novel—in the sense that the author views man as a mechanism helpless in the grasp of some superior force. Rather, Steinbeck denounces those who see men as merely mechanisms to be manipulated. Nor is this melodrama, as some have suggested, but tragedy—a tragedy grimmer than any about man destroyed by uncontrollable external forces, since it is about man destroyed by uncontrolled internal forces.

CHAPTER 7

End of a Dream

OF MICE AND MEN marks the end of the first period in Steinbeck's literary career in several ways. First, this was the work that brought him at last really impressive national recognition and substantial reward and thus brought him face to face with the problems of a man in the limelight. Like Danny in *Tortilla Flat*, Steinbeck had achieved a position from which there was no turning back. Secondly, *Of Mice and Men* is the book in which Steinbeck found at last the form he had been struggling for—the method of objective storytelling which is really a fictionalized play. All of Steinbeck's novels had contained extraneous material (like the "Caporal" episode in *Tortilla Flat*, in which the *paisanos* expressed out-of-character views). The short stories to be collected into *The Red Pony* perfectly blended form and content, but it was not until *Of Mice and Men* that Steinbeck achieved the same structural soundness in a complex narrative.

Thirdly, in this novel Steinbeck at last discovered how to present the point underlying *Cup of Gold* in a convincing, contemporary setting. Behind the piratical trappings of the first novel stalked the ironic perception that maturity means the destruction of dreams. Other dreamers had learned this lesson in Steinbeck's novels; but Henry Morgan had been the only Steinbeck hero to survive his disillusionment. George in *Of Mice and Men* is the first contemporary figure in a Steinbeck novel to "split" before the onslaught of civilization rather than go under. Steinbeck had at last found the figure that could disentangle the grail quest from the mists of legend and make its futility explicit in down-to-earth terms.

Of Mice and Men is Steinbeck's last novel to be directly influenced by Arthurian legend. In *The Grapes of Wrath*, the writer turns to Biblical traditions for his analogues. This change makes his allegories more generally comprehensible because of the wide familiarity with Biblical imagery. There is an "ivory tower" quality about even Steinbeck's most realistic novels before *The Grapes of Wrath;* and it was probably his months of living among the migrants that enabled him to shake off the lingering effects of the—to American eyes—somewhat remote myths that had long provided the framework for his novels.

Although other critics have not noted to what extent *Of Mice and Men* is an Arthurian story, the fundamental parallels— the knightly loyalty, the pursuit of the vision, the creation of a bond (shared briefly by Candy and Brooks), and its destruction by an at least potentially adulterous relationship— are there. They are, however, so concealed by the surface realism of the work that one unfamiliar with Steinbeck's previous Arthurian experiments would be hardly likely to notice them. The one obvious Arthurian hangover is George, who is not only remarkably loyal to his charge—the feeble-minded Lennie—but also remarkably pure.

George not only warns Lennie against the blandishments of Curley's wife, but is himself obviously impervious to her charms. While the other ranch hands are excited by her presence, George says only, "Jesus, what a tramp!" When invited to join the boys in a Saturday night trip to a neighboring town's "nice" whorehouse, George says that he "might go in an' set and have a shot," but "ain't puttin' out no two and a half." He excuses himself on the ground that he is saving money to buy a farm, but not even Galahad might have found it politic to profess chastity in a bunkhouse. George seems to have stepped, in fact, not out of Malory's Arthurian stories but Tennyson's. When he is told that Curley boasts of having his glove full of Vaseline in order to keep his hand soft for his wife, George says, "That's a dirty thing to tell around."

George is noticeably more critical of Curley's wife than Steinbeck is. *Of Mice and Men* is not so completely objective as *In Dubious Battle;* Steinbeck editorializes occasionally, for example, after the girl has been killed:

> . . . the meanness and the plannings and the discontent and the ache for attention were all gone from her face. She was very pretty and simple, and her face was sweet and young.

George shows no such sympathy, and it is important to notice that the author is more flexible than his character, because it is a sign that he is not being carried away by his vision as are the characters sometimes assumed to represent his viewpoint. The Arthurian flavor here is faint, but unmistakable. Like Jim Nolan, George is a last Galahad, dismounted, armed only with a fading dream, a long way from Camelot. Steinbeck is his historian, not his alter ego.

One does not need to justify a search for an allegory in *Of Mice and Men* since the author has spoken of the book as symbolic and microcosmic. Just what the universal drama enacted against a Salinas Valley backdrop may be is not, however, so obvious as first appears. Unquestionably it concerns a knight of low estate and a protégé who share a dream, a dream that cannot come true because the protégé lacks the mental capacity to be conscious enough to know his own strength or to protect himself from temptation.

At first glance, it appears that nature is the culprit and that this is an ironic, deterministic fable like Stephen Crane's "The Open Boat." It is an indifferent nature that makes men physically strong but mentally deficient; dreaming is man's only defense against a world he never made. "The best-laid schemes o' mice an' men aft agley," Burns said, providing Steinbeck with a title, because man is at the mercy of forces he cannot control which ruthlessly but indifferently destroy the illusions he has manufactured. The book may be read in this naturalistic manner, and those who speak of it as sentimental must think of it as an expression of Steinbeck's outraged compassion for the victims of chaotic forces.

Such a reading, however, does not do the story justice. If George stood helplessly by and saw Lennie destroyed, the novel might be called deterministic; but he doesn't. George has a will, and he exercises it to make two critical decisions at the end of the novel—to kill Lennie and to lie about it.

George could, of course, have killed Lennie simply to protect the giant brute from the mob; but, since Lennie doesn't know what is going on anyway, it is easy to oversentimentalize George's motives. Actually he has reasons of his own for pulling the trigger. Steinbeck makes it clear that George had tremendous difficulty bringing himself to destroy Lennie, although Lennie will not even know what has happened. What George is actually trying to kill is not Lennie, who is only a shell and a doomed one at that, but something in himself.

Peter Lisca points out that Lennie's need for George is obvious, but that George's need for Lennie, though less obvious, is as great. In his most candid appraisal of himself, George says, "I ain't so bright neither, or I wouldn't be buckin' barley for my fifty and found. If I was even a little bit smart, I'd have my own little place. . . ." He needs him, however, as more than just a rationalization for his own failure; for George not only protects but *directs* Lennie. Lennie doesn't speak unless George permits him to; and, in the fight in which Curley's hand is broken, Lennie refuses even to defend himself until George tells him to. George, of course, directs Lennie partly to protect him from committing acts he could not mentally be responsible for, but George is not a wholly altruistic shepherd. Another aspect of the relationship becomes apparent when George tells Slim that Lennie, "Can't think of nothing to do himself, but he sure can take orders." Since George gives the orders, Lennie gives him a sense of power.

One aspect of the dream that George repeatedly describes to Lennie also needs scrutiny. The ritual ("George's voice became deeper. He repeated his words rhythmically.") begins "Guys like us, that work on ranches, are the loneliest guys in the world. . . . They ain't got nothing to look ahead to" and continues "with us it ain't like that . . . because [here Lennie takes over from George] I got you to look after me, and you got me to look after you, and that's why." The dream not only gives a direction to their lives, but also makes them feel different from other people. Since this sense of difference can mean little to Lennie, it is part of the consolation George receives from the dream. George wants to be superior. With Lennie gone, his claim to distinction will be gone. Thus when George shoots Lennie, he is not destroying only the shared dream. He is also destroying the thing that makes him different and reducing himself to the status of an ordinary guy. He is obliged to acknowledge what Willy Loman in Arthur Miller's *Death of a Salesman*, for example, could never acknowledge but what Henry Morgan accepted when he turned respectable in *Cup of Gold*—his own mediocrity. George is much like Willy Loman; for he is forced to recognize the same self-deflating realization Biff Loman vainly tries to impress upon his father: he is a "dime a dozen." Because of their relationship, George has actually been able to remain as much a "kid" as Lennie; shooting him matures George in more than one way.

It is equally important that George lies to the posse after the shooting. If the experience had not matured him, he had here his opportunity for a grand gesture. He could either destroy himself along with Lennie and the dream or, by an impassioned confession, force his enemies to destroy him. George, who by Romantic standards has little left to live for, chooses to go on living and to say that he had to shoot Lennie in self-defense. Actually the maturing effect of the experience upon George has been apparent from the moment when, in reply to Candy's offer to help him carry out the dream, he says: "—I think I knowed from the very first. I think I know'd we'd never do her. He usta like to hear about it so much I got to thinking maybe we would." With Lennie gone, George will not try to keep the dream alive. When Slim leads George up toward the highway at the end of the novel, the wonder is not that George is badly shaken by his experience, but that he is alive at all.

Despite the grim events it chronicles *Of Mice and Men* is not a tragedy, but a comedy—which, if it were Shakespearean, we would call a "dark comedy"—about the triumph of the indomitable will to survive. This is a story not of man's defeat at the hands of an implacable nature, but of man's painful conquest of this nature and of his difficult, conscious rejection of his dreams of greatness and acceptance of his own mediocrity. Unfortunately, the allegory is less clear in the play version than in the novel, since Steinbeck, probably to provide a more effective curtain, eliminates George's last conversation with Slim and ends with the shooting of Lennie. The original ending would also probably have been too involved for playgoers to follow after experiencing the emotions engendered by the climactic episodes.

Lennie has been viewed sometimes as an example of Steinbeck's preoccupation with subhuman types; actually Lennie is not a character in the story at all, but rather a device like a golden coin in *Moby Dick* to which the other characters may react in a way that allows the reader to perceive their attitudes. So intensely focused upon the relationship between George and Lennie is the novel that the other characters are likely to be overlooked; yet each makes an important contribution to the narrative and provides a clue to Steinbeck's conception of the human condition.

The protest against racial discrimination and the treatment of the aged through the characters of Brooks and Candy needs no elaboration. The symbolism of Curley and his ill-fated bride is perhaps summed up in her statement that they married after she "met him out to Riverside Dance Palace that same night." There is a sordid echo of Fitzgerald and the "lost generation" here; for, like the Buchanans in *The Great Gatsby*, these are "careless people" who smash up things and "let other people clean up the mess." It is true that the girl is smashed up herself, but, unlike Curley, she did have dreams and disappointments. He simply, like the Buchanans, retreats into his "vast carelessness." The wife, not George, is the one in the novel who is destroyed when, instead of controlling her dreams, she allows them to control her; and Curley, not Lennie, is actually the willfully animalistic type.

The most interesting characters—except for George and Lennie—are Carlson and Slim, two other ranch hands, who have the last words in the novel. They are complements, symbolizing, on one hand, the insensitive and brutal; on the other, the kindly and perceptive. "Now what the hell ya suppose is eatin' them two guys?" are Carlson's words—the last in the book—as Slim and George sadly walk off for a drink. Undoubtedly this sums up Steinbeck's concept of an unperceptive world's reaction to the drama just enacted. The uncomprehending responses to his books had given Steinbeck sufficient grounds for being aware of this "practical" attitude and through Carlson he strikes back at the men to whom Doctor Burton in *In Dubious Battle* attributes the world's "wild-eyed confusion." But Steinbeck also suggests that such men have the last word.

This bitterly ironic view is expressed through the major incident involving Carlson: the shooting of Candy's old dog.

All Carlson can see about the dog is that "he don't have no fun . . . and he stinks to beat hell." He has no feelings about the animal, and, because his reactions are entirely physical, no concept that anyone else might have feelings about it. He is the same kind of man as the agitators Steinbeck condemned in *In Dubious Battle*—insensitive, violent, fanatical. This "practical" man's only contributions to the group are destructive.

To balance this destructive force, Steinbeck introduces and awards the next-to-last word to the jerkline skinner, Slim, the man who alone understands and tries to comfort George at the end of the novel. Steinbeck breaks his editorial silence, as he does in speaking of Curley's wife, to make it absolutely clear to the reader how Slim is to be regarded. "His ear heard more than was said to him," the author writes, "and his slow speech had overtones not of thought, but of understanding beyond thought." "His authority," the reader is told, "was so great that his word was taken on any subject, be it politics or love." What matters most, however, is the professional standing of this paragon:

> He moved with a majesty only achieved by royalty and master craftsmen. He was a jerkline skinner, capable of driving ten, sixteen, even twenty mules with a single line to the leaders. He was capable of killing a fly on the wheeler's butt with a bull whip without touching the mule.

The important thing about this passage is the emphasis placed upon skill and craftsmanship; here is the really "practical" man—not the callous boor, but the man who is able to do his job exceedingly well. We are to meet him again in *Cannery Row* and *The Wayward Bus*. It is notable that he is not a dreamer, but a doer. In another editorial aside that sets the tone for the whole book, Steinbeck points out that among other things with which the shelves where the ranch hands kept their personal belongings were loaded were "those Western magazines ranch men love to read and scoff at and secretly believe." Underneath the surface most men are not only dreamers, but unsuccessful dreamers; the real heroes are not these dreamers, but the doers. The heroic "doers," however, are not those who act only for personal aggrandizement, but those who try to do their best out of an affection for their craft and who feel compassionate rather than scornful toward the dreamers. With *Of Mice and Men,* Steinbeck himself unmistakably joins this class of craftsmen, for he not only shows compassion for the plight of the dreamer, but he accomplishes in the manner of a master craftsman his intention to sort out and evaluate the categories of men. Having mastered his craft, he was ready to execute his masterpiece.

CHAPTER 8

Adventures in the Long Valley

BEFORE TURNING to *The Grapes of Wrath*, we must pause to look at some shorter works Steinbeck had been producing during his "apprenticeship" period. Like other writers, he had found it difficult to sell distinctive and perceptive short stories to formula-ridden American magazines; finally in 1933 and 1934 the *North American Review* accepted four stories, including the first two parts of *The Red Pony*. After the success of *Tortilla Flat*, other magazines became interested, but Steinbeck could still place "The Snake" only in a Monterey newspaper. Not until *Of Mice and Men* and the benediction of the Book-of-the-Month Club firmly impressed his name upon the general public were his publishers willing to take a chance on the always risky venture of a collection of short stories. At last in 1938, however, *The Long Valley* appeared to provide a fitting climax to the formative period of Steinbeck's literary career.

It would be difficult and not really useful to establish the exact time and order of the writing of these stories since they are products of the same period and reflect the same interests as the early novels about California. The only one conspicuously different in content and tone from the others is "Saint Katy, the Virgin," and it resembles parts of *Cup of Gold*.

The other ten stories are all vignettes of life in the Salinas Valley. Several of them, in fact, are preparatory sketches for more ambitious works. "The Raid," for example, is an account of an experienced Communist agitator and his "trainee's" preparations for a workers' meeting; the two are prototypes of Mac and Jim in *In Dubious Battle* and the emphasis in the story is entirely—as it is partially in the novel—on the organizers' indifference to individuals and their religious devotion to a cause. Although the older man scoffs at "that religion stuff," it is obvious that both he and the young man are cultivating martyrdom. Since the story describes, however, only the apparently deliberately sought martyrdom of fanatics, it makes a faint impression beside the much more complex and terrifying novel employing similar characters.

"Breakfast," the slightest of the stories in *The Long Valley*, is nothing more than a sketch describing a family of cotton-pickers who share their simple meal with a stranger. Steinbeck, who comments that "there was some element of great beauty there that makes the rush of warmth when I think of it," later incorporated the incident almost unchanged into the twenty-second chapter of *The Grapes of Wrath*.

Two other stories are principally descriptive, but they depict terrifying rather than heart-warming events. "Flight," first printed in the collected volume, follows a young man from his initiation into manhood to his death. Mama Torres, looking at her nineteen-year-old son Pepe, feels that "it will be a nice thing to have a man in the house again." Her hopes, however, are frustrated; the only skill Pepe has developed is that of expertly throwing his dead father's switch-blade knife. When he is considered man enough to make his first journey into town alone, he celebrates by throwing the knife into a man who said names to him that he "could not allow." Most of the story describes his lonely flight to an inevitable death; and in this story Steinbeck comes closest to writing in the traditional naturalistic vein. Despite its brevity, "Flight" is strongly reminiscent of *An American Tragedy*, since Pepe, like Dreiser's Clyde Griffiths, is an impetuous but not too intelligent young man who is destroyed when a social situation places upon him responsibilities he is unequipped to assume.

Naturalistic elements also play a large role in "The Snake," a story reminiscent of the episode in *To a God Unknown* about the old man who makes nightly sacrifices to the setting sun. Steinbeck has commented in "About Ed Ricketts" that he wrote this incident of a woman's purchasing a male rattlesnake and watching it eat a rat just as it happened and that he didn't know what it meant himself. There is no reason not to believe him; the woman's behavior is one of those "naked things," irrational impulses that make people eternal enigmas.

The woman, however, like Lennie in *Of Mice and Men,* is important not so much for herself as for what she allows us to learn about another. The scientist from whom she purchases the snake "hated people who made sport of natural processes" and resents the pleasure the woman gets from seemingly identifying with the snake. Steinbeck's sympathy lies not with those who give free rein to irrational drives, but those who seek knowledge of the world they live in. "He could kill a thousand animals for knowledge," Steinbeck writes of the scientist, "but not an insect for pleasure"; and he says much the same of Doc in *Cannery Row.* That such scientists are not merely the detached, inhuman observers some emotional people claim is also illustrated by this story. Two weaknesses save the scientist from being a learning machine. He does want to be recognized as an individual. When the woman refuses to study a microscope slide he has made, he is annoyed. "Although answering questions bored him," Steinbeck writes, expressing a view that may explain a lot about some of his own behavior, "a lack of interest in what he was doing irritated him."

Although the scientist can, furthermore, be ruthlessly objective in dealing with other forms of life, he cannot gaze unblinkingly at certain human behavior. When the snake is about to eat the rat, the man cannot look at the intently watching woman. "If she's opening her mouth, I'll be sick," he thinks; "I'll be afraid." Steinbeck is aware that there are limits to the sensitive person's objectivity. It is probably this awareness that one's attitudes can be simultaneously scientific and emotional that has led to querulous complaints from sentimentalists that Steinbeck is a mechanist and from mechanists that he is a sentimentalist.

The compound of science and sentiment that enables him to be both outraged and yet unblinded by his rage at certain aspects of human behavior accounts for the effectiveness of the five ironic tales that are the most nearly conventional short stories in *The Long Valley.* Since these stories are too complex for exhaustive analysis if this study of all Steinbeck's fiction is to be kept within manageable bounds and since they are models of short story construction that should challenge the developing critic to make his own analyses, I shall suggest only briefly the way in which they are variations on the common theme of frustration.

"The Chrysanthemums" deals with a subject that, *In Dubious Battle* makes clear, especially infuriates Steinbeck: the manipulation of people's dreams for selfish purposes. Steinbeck perceived long before the revelations of Vance Packard's *The Hidden Persuaders* that the clever pitchman knows how to take callous advantage of others' suppressed feelings. Just as Mac in *In Dubious Battle* pets Anderson's dogs in order to win the man's confidence, so the repairman in "The Chrysanthemums" earns himself a meal by playing upon Elisa Allen's passionate affection for the flowers that symbolize her feeling of closeness to a rhythm of nature. His calculating exploitation of her secret feelings more than injures the woman; it drives her to distrust, to wish to hurt others, and to withdraw even further from human society and closer to the vegetable nature she feels in sympathy with. Underlying this simple tale is a theory about a major reason for the frequently deplored breakdown of communications in our time— people are suspicious of media that have so often been used to do long-range damage in order to produce short-term benefits.

In this story, the woman is hurt; in the others, women inflict hurts. The simplest and clearest of these is "The Vigilante," an unjustly neglected story of a man who has taken part in a lynching that belongs beside Faulkner's "Dry September" as an exposition of the contribution of boredom to violence. Most of the story simply describes the reactions of an individual after he has impetuously participated in an act of violence; but at the end, when he returns home, his wife accuses him, on the basis of the look on his face, of having been with a woman. When he looks in the mirror, he observes, "By God, she was right. . . . That's just exactly how I feel." Although the woman speaks only three times, she is characterized as a shrew whose suspicions make her husband's life a hell, and Steinbeck clearly implies that there is more behind the lynching of a Negro than race prejudice. Boredom and frustration seek outlets.

That frustration may, however, become a way of life is the thesis of "The Harness." In this depressing tale, it is disclosed after the death of a respected farmer's wife that she has held him in check in many ways, even making him wear a chest harness and elastic belt to improve his posture. His only relief from the discipline she has imposed upon him has been a week's fling once a year in San Francisco's brothels, and he has had to pay for this not only by behaving himself the rest of the time, but also by nursing her through long illnesses apparently resulting from her frustration at being unable to enthrall him completely.

After she dies, the husband attempts to throw off the yoke she has imposed upon him, but he has become so conditioned to her discipline that he cannot escape it. Like Pat Humbert in *The Pastures of Heaven,* he is a victim of a past that has made too strong a mark upon him to be effaced. Although he will not wear the physical harness again, he cannot throw off the "harness" the wife put upon his thinking. The really disturbing point of the story seems to be, however, not that the husband has become the captive of his dead wife, but that he really doesn't mind, because he can conceive of no other voice to listen to anyway. Bondage is here, as in many of Steinbeck's works, the penalty of ignorance.

An even more frightening bondage is depicted in "The White Quail." Mary Teller is one who does not wish to recognize, as Doc Burton tells Mac in *In Dubious Battle,* that "nothing stops," that change begins again as soon as something is established. Mary is not, however, like many of Steinbeck's characters, unconscious of her static attitude. She deliberately seeks to create an unchanging world. She will marry only a man who will allow her to build a garden she wants and to keep it absolutely unaltered. She knows, however, that she is insisting on an unchanging garden in order to keep out "the world that wants to get in, all rough and tangled and unkempt."

What she does not realize is that her efforts to build a stable world for herself—which may have been inspired by a terror of the uncertainties of child-bearing—have been made selfishly, sacrificing her husband to her lust for security. His reaction is not apparent until she identifies herself with a white quail that visits the garden and becomes terrified when a cat threatens the bird. She insists the cat be destroyed, but her husband instead shoots the quail. "I just wanted to scare it away," he says. He even calls himself "a dirty skunk" for killing "a thing she loved so much." At last, however, he breaks down shouting, "Oh, Lord, I'm so lonely." Killing the white quail symbolizes his desire to destroy the wife who has walled him out of her life. The ironic point is that one who succeeds in apparently defeating the ceaselessly changing order of nature by manufacturing security really only creates unending tensions (lest a cat representing the unkempt world creep in) and utter isolation for himself. The position obtained may not be worth the expense of spirit.

The same matter of the difficulty and desirability of maintaining a position is considered in "Johnny Bear." Steinbeck devotes much of this story to another of the "freaks," who are so often mistakenly considered his principal interest. It is especially apparent in this story that Steinbeck uses subnormal characters less as objects of interest in themselves than as vehicles for getting at otherwise hidden truths about others. The title character is a feeble-minded creature with a remarkable capacity for reproducing not only anything that he has heard, but the exact intonation of the speaker, although he understands nothing of what he mimics. For the whiskey he relishes, he will repeat what he has heard for the crowd in the town saloon. The story concerns his unwitting revelation of the secret of two sisters who are the town's symbols of respectability, a kind of community conscience. As one man explains: "They're what we tell our kids when we want to—well, to describe good people."

Johnny Bear reveals that one of these "good" people has hanged herself and that the other, the disciplinarian, has countenanced her sister's suicide in order to keep her illegitimate pregnancy secret. What is finally exposed to the reader and almost to the town through Johnny's agency is that the suicide is pregnant by a Chinese tenant farmer, something that if publicly known will, not only because of the "sin" but also the racial prejudices involved, destroy all sense of order in the town. Added to the warning of "The Harness" and "The White Quail" against starving people of affection in order to keep up a false front is one in "Johnny Bear" against putting faith in "good" people any more than in "good" causes. When an order is built upon a façade, the collapse of the façade invites chaos.

One curious element about "Johnny Bear" is that Steinbeck obviously expects the reader to recognize that it would be doubly degrading for the father of a white woman's illegitimate child to be Chinese. Most Californians would, of course, think that it was; but the fact that Steinbeck takes this attitude so much for granted seems a little inconsistent with his appeals for universal brotherhood. The treatment of the Chinese in this story also leads us to a scrutiny of what is in many ways the most peculiar story in *The Long Valley,* "The Murder," the first of Steinbeck's stories to be selected as among the year's best.

The story concerns a man of obviously "Anglo" stock who marries a Yugoslavian girl. A wonderful housekeeper, she fails to provide the desired social companionship. He begins to spend Saturday nights in town seeking the company of women of his own stock, but he is violently shaken when he accidentally returns home one night to find his wife bedded down with her cousin. He kills the cousin, beats the wife, and moves closer to town. Earlier his father-in-law had warned him, "Jelka is Slav girl. He's not like American girl. If he is bad, beat him. . . . He's not like a man that don't beat hell out of him." When Jim, relying on his own traditions, announces he won't beat Jelka, the father simply giggles. At the end of the story when Jelka asks, "Will you whip me any more—for this?" He says only, "No, not any more for this."

The story can, of course, be regarded simply as a study in comparative mores, but it is difficult to believe that Steinbeck could have thought most Americans would not read it as an illustration of racial superiority—and one wonders just what attracted those selecting the best stories to it instead of "The Red Pony." Steinbeck, it should be noted, was to speak callously again of non-Nordic peoples. For example, in his reports from the War Zone, collected in *Once There Was a War,* he talks about Arabs as "the dirtiest people in the world and among the smelliest." Even his treatment of Mexican natives, although compassionate, is often condescending for the natives of the *Forgotten Village* are a benighted lot, and the hero must run away to preserve himself.

Their Blood is Strong emphasizes even more strongly than *The Grapes of Wrath* that the migrants from Oklahoma have "good old names" and "are of English, German, and Scandinavian descent." Although Steinbeck thinks the migrant laborers imported earlier from abroad should be treated decently, he observes that these orientals and other non-Nordics have "invariably been drawn from a peon class" and the main point of his tract is that native Americans "will insist on a standard of living much higher than that which was accorded foreign 'cheap labor.'" There is in Steinbeck, as there was even more noticeably in the earlier California social protest writer, Frank Norris, a stronger notion of Nordic supremacy than one might expect. This element does not play a large role in Steinbeck's work, but it is important to recall its presence when assessing him as a mirror of American attitudes.

As for "The Murder," its point appears to be that people should be treated according to their own traditions even if we find them incomprehensible. Steinbeck may call for universal brotherhood, but he certainly does not call for a single universal pattern of behavior. Nor does he vitiate his argument by claiming like some idealists that we must not only accept but approve alien behavior.

✿   ✿   ✿

Another example of Steinbeck's conviction that accepting people as they are does not mean we must refrain from laughing at them if they behave absurdly is the delightful "St. Katy, the Virgin," the only one of his early short stories not about California. Steinbeck mentioned this tale as early as 1932, and it may have existed even before then since it is written in the mannered, facetious style he abandoned with the coming of the depression. It is perhaps regrettable that he abandoned this style, for he excels as a satirist.

This story reflects an attitude toward conventional religiosity much like that expressed in *Cup of Gold* and *To a God Unknown*. It parodies a traditional form of the Saint's life, the story of one converted from wickedness to piety, by recounting a pig's redemption. The main thrusts at religion are found, however, not in the ludicrous person of the pig but in incidental comments.

Throughout the story Steinbeck suggests that the church has become a symbol not of compassion but of social and material respectability. The first sentence explains that the church considers "bad" a man who "laughed too much at the wrong times and at the wrong people." The materialism of the church is satirized by Brother Paul's being blamed rather than commended for converting Katy. "There are plenty of Christians," the Abbot says with asperity; "This year there's a great shortage of pigs." An echo of Emerson's complaint against traditional Christianity—that "to aim to convert a man by miracles [rather than by beautiful sentiments] is a profanation of the soul"—is found in the story. Although the life of Katy subsequent to her conversion is "one long record of good deeds," the Brothers do not suppose that she may be a saint until she goes to the altar and "with a look of seraphic transport on her face, [spins] like a top on the tip of her tail for an hour and three-quarters."

The story culminates in a cynical burlesque of religious expediency. When Katy's having borne in her sinful days a litter of pigs (all of which she ate) raises some question about her being called "virgin," the problem is presented to "a fair-minded and vastly learned barber." He explains that there are two kinds of virgins. One is virginal by virtue of "a bit of tissue," but "this definition is a grave danger to the basis of our religion since there is nothing to differentiate between the Grace of God knocking it out from the inside or the wickedness of man from the outside." A great many others may be defined as virginal if the test of "virginity by intent" is used. "The committee went away satisfied," Steinbeck explains; "Katy had without doubt been a virgin by intent." Without belaboring the satire, we need only observe that to the scientifically trained mind there could be no more dubious practice than defining terms to mean what one wants them to mean rather than what the evidence will justify. The fathers seeking to sanctify Katy more nearly resemble the Communist agitators who justify their means by the goodness of their cause than Doctor Burton, who wants to "see the whole picture—as nearly as I can."

❋   ❋   ❋

The Red Pony should be considered apart from the rest of *The Long Valley,* since it is more nearly a brief episodic novel than a group of stories. While each of its four parts can be read separately, together they tell a unified story of a child's growth from selfish ignorance to compassionate enlightenment as his own experiences teach him to see the world, not as he wishes it to be, but as it is. In the third episode, Billy Buck, the ranch hand, tells young Jody that the only way to learn a thing is by being in on it right from the start, since "nobody can tell you anything." The four stories tell what the boy learns by being in on things from the start.

At the beginning of the first story, "The Gift," Jody is a child not only in the sense of being innocent of any knowledge of the world, but also in the sense of being completely controlled by others. The degree of his dependence is repeatedly stressed: "It didn't occur to him to disobey the harsh note" of the triangle calling him to breakfast; "Jody obeyed [his father] in everything without questions of any kind"; "Punishment would be prompt both at school and at home" if he had lied to get away from school. There are compensations, however, for this dependent status; Jody lives in a world of certainties and believes implicitly in the wisdom of those he obeys.

As the story opens, however, Jody feels "an uncertainty in the air, a feeling of change and of loss and of the gain of new and unfamiliar things." The first gain is that of a red pony Jody's father buys him; possession of and responsibility for the pony is the first step toward Jody's becoming an adult, toward his differentiation from the mass represented by the boys who come to admire the pony: "Before today Jody had been a boy, dressed in overalls and a blue shirt—quieter than most, even suspected of being a little cowardly. And now he was different. . . . [The other boys] knew that Jody had been miraculously lifted out of equality with them, and had been placed over them," because he has become a horseman.

With maturity comes disillusionment. The story is built chiefly around the ranch hand Billy Buck's promises to Jody. He promises first, when Jody is hesitant about leaving the pony out in the corral on a sunny day during a rainy season, that "it won't rain" and that, if it does, he will put the pony in. "Billy Buck wasn't wrong about many things," Steinbeck comments, because if Jody's faith is to be preserved, "He couldn't be." But this time he is; it does rain and Billy does not put the pony in but seeks refuge for himself on a neighboring ranch. "You said it wouldn't rain," Jody says accusingly to Billy, who replies that it's hard to tell at this time of the year. Steinbeck comments, "His excuse was lame. He had no right to be fallible, and he knew it."

The pony does catch cold, but Billy says that "he'll be all right in the morning." But he isn't. He grows worse. When his condition becomes serious, Jody asks about it. Billy does not want to tell the truth, but does, realizing "he couldn't be wrong three times." Later when Jody observes that the pony is very sick, Billy thinks a long time about what to say. "He nearly tossed off a careless assurance," the author explains, "but he saved himself in time." He cannot save the pony, though; it flees into a meadow at last and dies. When buzzards attack the carcass, Jody manages to grab one of them that stares at him "impersonal and unafraid and detached" even as he kills it. Jody's father chides him and asks if he doesn't know that the buzzard didn't kill the pony. Jody does, of course; he is simply practicing displacement, as he has earlier when he threw a clod at an unoffending but disgustingly healthy dog. He has learned that man cannot always vent his feelings directly on what has hurt him; he has also learned that nature is impersonal, no respecter of human wishes. The most important thing he has learned, however, is that the human beings he trusted implicitly are fallible and that even those who love us sometimes have only the alternatives of telling us something unpleasant or lying to us. He can never be a completely naive or dependent child again.

As the second story, "The Great Mountains," begins, we find that the once trusting Jody has become cruel and callous. He irrationally tortures a long-suffering dog and equally irrationally kills a thrush. Then he hides the bird's body to avoid telling the truth. "He didn't care about the bird, or its life," Steinbeck writes, "but he knew what the older people would say if they had seen him kill it; he was ashamed of their potential opinion." He is no longer respectful of adults, but he fears them. He has graduated to that intermediate state between childhood and manhood where one's principal guide to conduct is fear of public opinion, a state beyond which many, of course, never advance. Like fearful people, too, Jody has reached a state where he does not wish to accept responsibility. When an old man approaches him, he abruptly turns and runs to the house for help.

The old man is the central figure in this story. He has lived as a child on the land where the Tiflin ranch is, and he has come home to die now that he is too old to work. Jody's father unsympathetically refuses to let him stay; he compares him to an old horse "who ought to be shot." Only Jody talks to the old man and learns that he had once visited with his father the great mountains that Jody much admires, but that he remembers nothing of them except that it was "quiet and nice" there. Jody also learns that the old man's most prized possession is a rapier that he has inherited from his father. The next morning both the old man and the superannuated horse that Jody's father compared him to have disappeared; they have been seen heading towards the great mountains. Jody discovers that of his possessions the old man has taken only the rapier into this place that he remembers as "quiet and nice." As Jody thinks of the old man, he is full of "a nameless sorrow." This sorrow seems to be his recognition that adults, too, have their problems, that they become worn out, useless and unwanted, and frustrated by an indifferent nature. If youth, as he has learned earlier, has its tragedies, so does old age. His sympathies have been broadened.

"The Promise," the third story, opens with Jody conscious of the hurt feelings of the adults he associates with, and he himself is treated in a more adult manner. His father promises him a colt to replace the red pony if he will take one of the mares to be bred, earn the stud fee, tend the mare until she is ready to deliver (nearly a year), and then train the colt. Jody promises and finds himself "reduced to peonage for the whole late spring and summer." His relationship with the adults has subtly changed. Billy Buck will do everything he can to deliver the colt safely, but "won't promise anything." Jody endures the long wait (a kind of knightly ordeal), but at the end tragedy strikes again. Something goes wrong with the delivery, and Billy must kill the mare to save the colt.

During the tense moments of the tragic delivery, two other things happen: Jody, who used to obey automatically, refuses to obey until cursed, and Billy Buck for the first time in the stories loses his temper with the boy.

Jody is now irretrievably entered into the frustrating land of adult emotions and defeats. He has learned, furthermore, that just as man is fallible, so is nature. Although its operations continue indifferent to man's wishes, these operations are far from perfect. Nellie has delivered colts successfully before, but this time a hitch develops. Old life must sometimes be sacrificed not just because it has become useless (as in "The Great Mountains") but in order to make possible new. Nobody is at fault; the system is just not flawless. Jody has gotten what he wanted, but he has also learned what sacrifices men must sometimes make to achieve their ends.

The last story, "The Leader of the People," although added later, serves to round out the history of Jody's maturing. The story is skillfully connected with "The Promise" by Jody's first use in the narrative of the profanity he has picked up from Billy at the end of the preceding story. When he says, "I hope it don't rain until after I kill them damn mice," he looks over his shoulder "to see whether Billy had noticed the mature profanity," but Billy makes no comment.

The story is built around a visit from Jody's maternal grandfather, who led a group of emigrants westward in pioneering days. Jody's father does not look forward to the visit because of the old man's unending talk about his great experience. "He just goes on and on, and he never changes a word in the things he tells," he complains. Mrs. Tiflin replies quietly, "That was the big thing in father's life. He led a wagon train clear across the plains to the coast, and when it was finished, his life was done. It was a big thing to do, but it didn't last long enough."

When the old man arrives, he begins talking again. Although Jody listens enthusiastically, there is tension in the air. The climax comes when Jody's father, thinking the old man cannot hear him, asks with irritation, "Why does he have to tell [the stories] over and over? He came across the plains. All right! Now it's finished. Nobody wants to hear about it over and over." This time the old man does overhear the remarks, and his spirit is broken. "Don't be sorry, Carl," he tells his son-in-law, "an old man doesn't see things sometimes. Maybe you're right. The crossing is finished. Maybe it should be forgotten, now it's done." Disconsolately he sits on the porch. Jody remains loyal to him, and in the course of their conversation, the old man's real tragedy comes out. He has not, it turns out, simply wished to reminisce about the old days to glorify himself. "I tell these old stories," he tells Jody, "but they're not what I want to tell. I only know how I want people to feel when I tell them. . . . It wasn't getting here that mattered, it was movement and westering. . . . Then we came down to the sea, and it was done. That's what I should be telling instead of stories."

The tragedy is not just that the old man's job was finished too soon—that "there's a line of old men along the shore hating the ocean because it stopped them"—but even more that he is unable to communicate the feelings that motivated his generation to the younger generation. From him Jody learns that just as nature is fallible, so it too, like man, has its limits, wears out, offers no new frontiers. Jody also learns something even more important; he learns that the reasons why "nobody can tell you anything" is that experience is difficult to communicate. The intent may be there, but words fail to convey it, so that he who would inspire the young may seem just a long-winded old man.

Jody also shows that he has learned even more than these things. After hearing the old man, he offers to make him a lemonade. When his mother suggests that he wants to make one for the old man so that he can have one himself, he says, "No, ma'am, I don't want one." She supposes him sick; then recognizes that he wishes to do something genuinely altruistic. Small as this gesture is, it shows us that Jody has learned compassion—that he has truly emerged into adulthood since he has learned that the only way to deal with the fallibility and the limitations of both man and nature is to be compassionate.

The morals are not so obvious in the stories as in this explanation; Steinbeck has succeeded in this work in so fusing his form with his content that the complex "message" of the narrative is never forced nor obtrusive. Yet there is no wasted word in the chronicle. In his depiction of a young man's emergence into compassionate adulthood by his painful learning through four personal experiences of the fallibility of man, the wearing out of man, the unreliability of nature, and the exhaustion of nature, Steinbeck succeeds in doing what the old man failed to do—make the reader "feel" when he speaks.

CHAPTER 9

The Education of the Heart

STEINBECK'S greatest success at making people feel as he wished them to feel came with *The Grapes of Wrath* (1939), which Alexander Cowie describes in *The Rise of the American Novel* as "a brilliant and powerful synthesis" of most of the new features that have any value in the fiction of the seminal period between the two World Wars. Steinbeck has written nothing else as successful as this novel, nor does it seem likely he will. Few writers, however, have even written one such work—one that looking back we can see marks not only the high point of its author's career but the close of an era in American history and literature.

The Grapes of Wrath has been more often discussed than any other of Steinbeck's novels. The story of its reception— the adulation it inspired in many readers and its bitter denunciations by partisan politicians—has often been told; writers about contemporary fiction have often praised it and quarreled with it. There would seem to be little new to say about the novel, especially since it has attracted probably as large an audience as any novel about a serious contemporary theme. Nevertheless, certain misconceptions about the work persist even after twenty years, and it is with these that anyone seeking to do justice to Steinbeck must deal.

The intercalary chapters (often simply referred to as "interchapters") have long disturbed readers accustomed to conventional narrative forms. Steinbeck's method of interrupting his main narrative with material that does not add directly to the history of the Joad family especially upsets those who think a storyteller's duty is to get on with the story or those fanatics about "organic form" who are neurotically indisposed against shifts in style and subject. Perceptive critics have already pointed out that these inter-chapters are not disgressions, and Peter Lisca in *The Wide World of John Steinbeck* discusses at length the way in which the inter-chapters are related to episodes in the Joad story not only by repetitions of general themes but by carefully planned repeating of specific details; one should turn, therefore, to his account for an understanding of how artfully the book is put together. It is enough to say here that generally each chapter of the Joad story is paired with the preceding intercalary chapter and that both make the same point—one about conditions generally and one about how they specifically affected the Joads.

Although Steinbeck nowhere in *The Grapes of Wrath* discusses the method he is using, he explains, as Lisca points out, the conscious literary theory behind his procedure in a preface to a book containing still pictures from his film, *The Forgotten Village*. Commenting upon the problems that had to be solved in making this motion picture about the introduction of scientific medicine to a remote, superstition-ridden Mexican village, Steinbeck writes:

> A great many documentary films have used the generalized method, that is, the showing of a condition or an event as it affects a group of people. . . . In *The Forgotten Village* we reversed the usual process. Our story centered on one family in one small village. We wished our audience to know this family very well, and incidentally to like it, as we did. Then, from association with this little personalized group, the larger conclusion concerning the racial group could be drawn with something like participation.

In *The Grapes of Wrath*, however, Steinbeck did not take a chance on one method or the other, but used both in an effort to leave nothing undone that might put his point across. The Joad story centers, like *The Forgotten Village*, around one family, while the "generalized method" is used in the inter-chapters. By employing this double method, Steinbeck also did what he could to protect himself against the attacks some people launched against the book. By presenting the problems he was concerned with in terms of their effect upon an individual family, he forced his readers to visualize the problems as they affected particular persons and denied them the consolation of the sociology textbook that treats depressed groups in numbers too large to be individually meaningful.

On the other hand, by using the generalized method, he denied in advance the charge that the history of the Joads was unique. By making what happened to the Joads representative of general situations he depicted, he avoided precisely the error made by some who attempted to "answer" *The Grapes of Wrath* by presenting a unique case and implying it was typical.[1] In the inter-chapter, Steinbeck found exactly the device he needed to make his novel simultaneously a general and an intensely personal history of the travails of a culture in transition.

There is a more fundamental misunderstanding of the book than that resulting from puzzlement over the function of the inter-chapters. Many early reviewers compared the novel to *Uncle Tom's Cabin,* and this comparison is still made occasionally, although it shows little real appreciation of the distinctive qualities of either book. While it is true that Mrs. Stowe and Steinbeck both attempt to arouse people about a contemporary evil, they take quite different attitudes toward the nature of these evils and the proper remedies. Mrs. Stowe wrote in a truly revolutionary spirit, advocating the abolition of a system of political bondage, because, as she makes clear in her conclusion, she believed the system inherently evil. Even if the evils were rarely observed, she argued that the system could not exist without them and must be destroyed. She wrote, in more than one sense of the terms, a black-and-white story, based on a strongly teleological concept of virtue and designed to threaten those who persisted in an anti-Christian course with divine retribution.

Steinbeck, however, always deeply distrustful of both teleology and revolutions, sought reforms in an economic system, the present managers of which were in danger of being ousted because they had failed to solve crucial problems of distribution and expansion. He did not argue against the existing system, but argued rather that, since its evils were extensive, it must be overhauled. He understood, even if he could not sympathize with, the views of both sides; and he wrote a novel based on a non-teleological concept of the sur-

vival of the fittest, threatening those who persisted in op-
pressing the less fortunate with destruction at the hands of
the aroused oppressed. Ironically, it was not Mrs. Stowe but
writers like George Fitzhugh, who attacked Northern "wage-
slavery" in their defense of the patriarchal system of slavery,
who foreshadowed some of Steinbeck's arguments. The important point is, that to be understood, Steinbeck must be read
as a reformer, not a revolutionary. He writes in the tradition
of Swift, not Tom Paine; and his forebodings were prompted
by biological not theological considerations.

There is also a conspicuous difference between the oppressed in the two novels. Uncle Tom is represented to the
reader from his first appearance as a paragon of virtue:
"nothing could exceed the touching simplicity, the child-like
earnestness of his prayer, enriched with the language of
Scripture, which seemed so entirely to have wrought itself
into his being, as to have become a part of himself." His first
action is to sacrifice himself so that other slaves on the plan-
tation may be spared. Mrs. Stowe's powerful tract is, thus, as
far as its principal figure is concerned, static; for, while things
happen to Uncle Tom, there is nothing left to happen within
him. The pathos of the novel rises, like the power of *Othello,*
from the spectacle of virtue suffering at the hands of demented power.

Apparently many people, especially those who talk about
Steinbeck's sentimentalization of the underprivileged, think
that *The Grapes of Wrath* is the same kind of novel, but they
have not read it carefully. Steinbeck is not blind to the defects
of the Joads; he shows clearly that he writes about a group
of thoughtless, impetuous, suspicious, ignorant people. They
appropriate a neighbor's property without bothering to find
out whether he has abandoned it (59-59);* Uncle John "when
he wants pig he wants a whole pig, an' when he's through, he

---

* So that it will be easy to follow the argument here outlined through
the long novel, page references to quotations from *The Grapes of Wrath*
are given. These may prove especially useful since the pagination of
three readily available editions of this novel—the original Viking Press
edition, the Modern Library edition, and the Compass Books paperbound edition—are the same.

don't want no pig hangin' around" (40); the children are ignorant of the operation of flush toilets and ashamed to admit their ignorance (411); and Pa will only believe that the manager of the Weedpatch camp is "a-snootin' an' a-smellin' aroun'" (418); the migrants respond to the greatest menace of their period only with laughter: "they was a newsreel with them German soldiers kickin' up their feet—funny as hell" (447). They are quick tempered (Tom killed a man in a drunken brawl), and it is implied in Tom's first conversation with Casy and in the fifth chapter that the present plight of the tenant farmers is the result of their fatuous optimism and stubbornly proud refusal to leave unproductive land in spite of increasing debt and poverty: "Ever' year I can remember, we had a good crop comin' an' it never come" (37,—*see also* 42-53).

These people are not lovable and long-suffering; and Steinbeck does not argue that they are virtuous, but simply that they are human, as their oppressors refuse to recognize: "Them goddam Okies got no sense and no feeling. They ain't human," a filling station attendant in Needles says. "A human being wouldn't live like they do. . . . They ain't a hell of a lot better than gorillas" (301). Throughout the book there are references to the way the Okies are taunted by law enforcement officers and schoolchildren.

Steinbeck's non-teleological thinking is apparent in his unvarnished portrait of the unloveliness of the Okies; something should be done about the migrants' situation, he maintains, not because for any preconceived reasons it *shouldn't* exist, but because its existence menaces the health of the culture. Steinbeck does not wish the "have-nots" to destroy and supplant the "haves"; he wishes the "haves" to expand their system to offer its benefits to the "have-nots." He argues against acquired selfishness, not inherent evil, and he recognizes that since neither side in the quarrel has any monopoly on vice or virtue, the migrants, as symbolized by the Joads, must also change if they are to survive. What he has written, therefore, is not a *static* novel about long-suffering Jobs, but a *dynamic* novel about people who learn that survival depends upon their adaptability to new conditions.

The point that the novel tells a dynamic story about learning to change brings us to the third and apparently most
widespread misconception about it. In the final chapter, Ma
Joad leads the remnants of her "fambly" from their flood-
engulfed box-car to a dry barn on high land; there Rosasharn,
whose baby has been stillborn, feeds from her breast a man
on the point of death who can take no other nourishment.
Although it would seem that only the prurient, who have
missed the whole point that the plight of the migrants is really
desperate, could object to accepting this poignant scene
literally, the tableau has been a bone of contention since the
novel appeared.

Among the early reviewers, Clifton Fadiman wrote in the
New Yorker "the ending is the tawdriest kind of fake symbolism." A more studied objection was made in 1946 in *The
Novel and the World's Dilemma* by Edwin Berry Burgum,
who attributed the last scene to "a meretricious desire to
italicize the action," since he felt the gesture could only be
symbolic and no preparation had been made for such symbolism. A French critic argues[2] that the novel ends on "a purely poetic image which in no way brings the plot to a conclusion," and such an influential volume as James Hart's *Ox-
ford Companion to American Literature* still announces that
Steinbeck fails to complete the story of *The Grapes of Wrath*,
"the value of whose conclusion is purely symbolic." Thus it
is charged either that the conclusion does not really conclude
anything or is not prepared for by any over-all allegorical
structure in the novel. My thesis is that neither of these charges
is true and that the Joad story in *The Grapes of Wrath* is, like
The Red Pony, a consistent allegory that is concluded logically
and fittingly by Rosasharn's gesture.

It is true that in a sociological sense the novel is unfinished,
because Steinbeck does not tell us whether the migrants survive or disappear. He did not, however, know what the outcome of their struggles would be when he wrote; and he was
writing a literary allegory and not a sociological prophecy.
He did imply that the actions of the reader might have a bear-
ing upon the outcome of the situation, since he actually con-
fronted him in several of the final inter-chapters with the

same proposition that Prospero does in the "Epilogue" to
Shakespeare's *The Tempest*:

> Now my charms are all o'erthrown,
> And what strength I have's mine own,
> Which is most faint. Now 'tis true
> I must be here confin'd by you,
> Or sent to Naples. . . .
>
> .   .   .   .
>
> As you from crimes would pardon'd be,
> Let your indulgence set me free.

Steinbeck makes a similar plea in the twenty-fifth chapter
of his novel when he speaks of the understanding and knowledge and skill of the men who make California fruitful and
then describes as "a crime . . . that goes beyond denunciation
. . . a failure . . . that topples all our success" allowing children
to die in the midst of rotting plenty. The solution of this problem he leaves squarely to the conscience of the reader, as he
should, since a novel is art—an ordering of reality—and not a
sociological prescription. It should be recalled that even in
The Tempest, although Prospero's restoration is left to the
good will of the audience, one important matter has already
been settled when Prospero has learned to abjure magic and
the desire for revenge and to forgive even those who have
treated him unnaturally. Out of their tempestuous experiences
the Joads learn a lesson remarkably similar to that the more
articulate Prospero in his final speech challenges the audience
to learn also.

The story of the Joads, in so far as it concerns the novelist,
is also completed in the barn, for this book is not the tale of the
family's quest for security (which, as Shakespeare suggests,
cannot be achieved entirely by one's self), but of their education, which is shown to be completed by the final scene.

What "education"?—the education of the heart, one that
results in a change from their jealously regarding themselves
as an isolated and self-important family unit to their regarding themselves as part of a vast human family that, in Casy's
words, shares "one big soul ever'body's a part of" (33). The
book is not so much concerned with the frustrating physical

migration described as with an accompanying spiritual movement similar to that celebrated in Whitman's "Passage to India."

Casy, the former preacher, has already speculated upon the idea of the brotherhood of all men before the novel begins, although he cannot formulate it clearly. He finds it difficult to explain his idea that "maybe it's all men an' all women we love" (32), because "fella gets use' to a way a thinkin', it's hard to leave" (69). When, however, he finds confirmation of his theory in Muley Graves's statement, "If a fella's got somepin to eat an' another fella's hungry—why the first fella ain' got no choice." He recognizes it, although he is obliged to say, "Muley's got a-holt of somepin, an' it's too big for him, an' it's too big for me" (66). The difficulty of clarifying his new idea had been evident when he and Tom reached the deserted Joad house and Casy confessed, "If I was still a preacher I'd say the arm of the Lord had struck. But now I don't know what's happened" (55). Still he is able to exemplify his new ideas when he replies to Ma Joad's statement that cutting pork is women's work, "It's all work. . . . They's too much of it to split up to men's or women's work" (146).

When Casy finally learns what he does mean in a California jail, he explains his ideas in the form of a parable illustrating the effectiveness of unified action. Speaking of the inmates, he says,

> "Well, they was nice fellas, ya see. What made 'em bad was they needed stuff. An' I begin to see then. It's need that makes all the trouble. I ain't got it worked out. Well, one day they give us some beans that was sour. One fella started yellin' an' nothin' happened. He yelled his head off. Trusty comes along an' looked in an' went on. Then another fella yelled. Well, sir, then we all got yellin'. And we all got on the same tone. . . . Then somepin happened! They come a-runnin', and they give us some other stuff to eat—give it to us. Ya see?" (521-22).

But at the moment, Tom Joad doesn't and Casy observes, "Maybe I can't tell you. . . . Maybe you got to find out" (522). The novel tells the story of the Joads' "finding out."

They are a difficult case. *The Grapes of Wrath* is not a tale

of the conversion of the susceptible. The family's haughty, isolated attitude at the beginning of the story is summed up in
Tom's remark to a friendly truck driver, "Nothin' ain't none
of your affair except skinnin' this here bull-bitch along, and
that's the least thing you work at" (18). Tom is no thinker.
When Casy tells him "They's gonna come a thing that's gonna
change the whole country," he simply replies, "I'm still layin'
my dogs down one at a time" (237). Uncle John, who has
been responsible for the death of his wife, has come closest
to understanding that there is something beyond the family,
but he has attributed the failure of his isolated pride to "sin"
and indulged in disorganized acts of charity, so that, as Pa
explains, he "give away about ever'thin' he got, an' still he
ain't very happy" (92).

Ma, whom Steinbeck describes as "the citadel of the
family" (100), views the trip to California entirely in terms
of personal success. She ponders, "I wonder—that is, if we all
get jobs an' all work—maybe we can get one of them little
white houses" (124). Although she burns her souvenirs to cut
herself off from her past (148), Ma does so because she thinks
primarily of herself as important to the family. When Tom
asks her if she is "scared a goin' to a new place?" and if she
has thought about the life there, she replies:

> "No, I ain't. . . . Up ahead, they's a thousan' lives we might
> live, but when it comes it'll on'y be one . . . it's just the road
> goin' by for me. . . . All the rest'd get upset if I done any
> more'n that. They all depen' on me jus' thinkin' about that"
> (168-69).

When Ma threatens Pa with the jack-handle to prevent the
party's splitting up, she acts to preserve the integrity of the
family, arguing:

> "What we got lef' in the world? . . . All we got is the family
> unbroke. Like a bunch of cows, when the lobos are ranging,
> stick all together. I ain't scared while we're all here, all that's
> alive, but I ain't gonna see us bust up" (230-31).

Although the Joads are neighborly toward the Wilsons—as
Sairy Wilson says, "People needs—to help" (192)—Ma still
seeks rationalizations that will bring the Wilsons into the

family rather than make assistance to them seem help to just anyone. "We got almost a kin bond," she tells Sairy, "Grampa, he died in your tent" (227), and she still insists that Casy not write the note to be pinned on Grampa's body, because he "wan't no kin" (195).

The family disintegrates, though, in spite of Ma's brave efforts and bold protests. The dog is killed on the highway (177); Grampa dies of a stroke before the family leaves Oklahoma (188), and Granma dies during the trip across the California desert (311). Although each of these deaths symbolizes an inability to adjust to changed conditions the migration imposes upon the family, they do not challenge the basic unity of the family. Ma is more severely shaken by the departure of Noah, which causes her to observe, after a long silence, "Family's fallin' apart . . . I don' know. Seems like I can't think no more" (294) and by the disappearance of Rose of Sharon's husband, Connie Rivers (371-72), which is especially an affront to tradition, both because the young couple have already threatened the family's security with talk of striking out for themselves (224) and because, by Connie's defection, a potential family unit is shattered as it is forming.

Ma's family pride is also shaken in other ways. She is disturbed by the California border patrolman from whom she first hears the term "Okie" and who tells her, "We don't want none of you settlin' down here" (291). Then she is upset by the vigilance committee which tells the family, "We ain't gonna have no goddamn Okies in this town" (383). Despite these affronts to her dignity and her insistence on sharing with the Wilsons over their protests, she still thinks primarily in terms of the family unit. Her reaction upon arriving in Bakersfield is that "the fambly's here" (311) and in the encounter with the vigilantes she counsels Tom to do nothing because "the fambly's breakin' up" (381).

The first significant change in the family's attitude occurs in the Weedpatch government camp where the Wallaces share their work with Tom and the self-governing arrangement makes the Joads feel like decent people again. Evaluating her recent experiences, Ma says, ". . . in Needles, that police, he done somepin' to me, made me feel mean. Made me feel ashamed. An' now I ain't ashamed. These folks is our folks. . . . Why, I feel like people again" (420), but she prefaces her remarks with the reminder, "We're Joads," and she still talks of the little white cottage. At the camp the Joads meet people who do not think of co-operation as "charity," while another lesson in co-operation is taught Ruthie by the children who ostracize her when she tries to dominate their games (434). All is not harmony, however, at Weedpatch, as is shown by the religious bigot's attack upon Rosasharn and the report of a garbage fight between the women. Pa Joad, too, is still far from converted to Casy's way of thinking. "I can't starve so's you can get two bits," he tells another man in a quarrel over taking others' jobs for lower wages (463).

The atmosphere at the government camp, where, as one man observes, "We're all a-workin' together" (488), is in striking contrast to the atmosphere at the Hooper Ranch, where the prevailing mode of thought is epitomized in the checker's remark that putting holes in the bottom of buckets "keeps people from stealing them" (506). It is here that Ma observes, "I'm learnin' one thing good . . . if you're in trouble or hurt or need—go to poor people. They're the only ones that'll help—the only ones" (513-14). The Joads still think of help, however, as help in maintaining the family. When Casy, now a labor organizer, pleads with Tom to support a strike against the Hooper Ranch, Tom says, "Pa wouldn' do it . . . I know 'im. He'd say it was none of his business. . . . Think Pa's gonna give up his meat on account a other fellas?" (524).

A crisis is precipitated at this ranch by Tom's impetuously disregarding the family's best interests and killing the man who has killed Casy. He decides that he must run away, because, as he tells Ma, he "can't go puttin' this on you folks." Ma retorts angrily, ". . . goin' away ain't gonna ease us. It's gonna bear us down. They was a time when we was on the lan'. They was a boundary to us then . . . an' we was always one thing—we was the fambly—kinda whole and clear. An' now we ain' clear no more. . . . We're crackin' up, Tom. There ain't no fambly now" (536). She pleads with him to stay and he agrees. The family does leave the ranch, but to protect Tom, not in protest against the strikebreaking. Ma's suspicion of any idea beyond that of loyalty to the family appears in her remark when Tom protests, "I got to go," "You can't. . . . They wouldn' be no way to hide out. You couldn' trus' nobody. But you can trus' us. We can hide you, an' we can see you get to eat while your face gets well" (545-46).

A major change in attitude comes at last in the final interview between Tom and Ma. Ruthie has undone the family by boasting about it; in a childish quarrel, she has revealed that her brother is a killer, who is hiding out nearby. Ma realizes that Tom must go. While hiding, Tom has been thinking over Casy's ideas, and when his mother says that she is worried that she may not know what has become of him, he tells her:

> "Well, maybe like Casy says, a fella ain't got a soul of his own, but on'y a piece of a big one—an' then . . . it don' matter. Then I'll be aroun' in the dark. I'll be ever'where you look. Wherever they's a fight so hungry people can eat, I'll be there. . . . An' when our folks eat the stuff they raise an' live in the houses they build—why, I'll be there" (572).

Tom has thus lost his clannishness and replaced it with the concept that one must give help to anyone who needs it. Gradually the family comes to share this concept.

Pa's learning the lesson of co-operation is shown in his action of building a dam to hold the flood-water out of the cotton-pickers' camp; he cries, "We can do her if ever'body helps" (595), although there is no indication that his idea of co-operation goes as far beyond an immediate situation as Tom's. Uncle John, too, finally breaks with tradition in a negative way in order to teach the world a lesson, when instead of giving Rosasharn's stillborn child the kind of family burial Pa had talked of when Grampa died (190), he sets it adrift in a creek, saying, "Go down in the street an' rot an' tell 'em that way. That's the way you can talk. Don' even know if you was a boy or a girl. Ain't gonna find out" (609).

Ma's acceptance of the idea of a responsibility that extends beyond the family after her last meeting with Tom is shown in her conversation with a neighbor, whom she thanks for help during Rosasharn's birth agonies:

> The stout woman smiled "No need to thank. Ever'body's in the same wagon. S'pose we was down. You'd a give us a han'."

"Yes," Ma said, "we would."

"Or anybody."

"Or anybody. Use'ta be the fambly was fust. It ain't so now. It's anybody. Worse off we get, the more we got to do" (606).

But this is simply a speech. It accepts the spirit of Casy's ideas of universal brotherhood, but it does not translate them into action. Some gesture must be made to indicate that the education has really transformed the family's behavior.

The opportunity to make this gesture occurs in the barn where the family discovers the famished man. Ma's unstated suggestion that Rosasharn give her milk to the starving man is only carrying into practice the idea that "worse off we get, the more we got to do." Having come to the barn with almost nothing, the family, through Rosasharn, gives the one thing— and one of the most intimate things—it has to offer. The tableau does not halt an unfinished story; it marks the end of the story Steinbeck had to tell about the Joads. Their education is completed. They have triumphed over familial prejudices. What happens to them now depends upon the ability of the rest of society to learn the same lesson they have already learned. Steinbeck himself expresses the point of view that underlies the whole novel when he writes:

This you may say of man—when theories change and crash, when schools, philosophies, when narrow dark alleys of thought, national, religious, economic, grow and disintegrate, man reaches, stumbles forward, painfully, mistakenly sometimes. Having stepped forward, he may slip back, but only half a step, never the full step back (204-5).

The Joads have taken a painful step forward. The book is neither riddle nor tragedy—it is an epic comedy of the triumph of the "holy spirit." The Joads have not yet been saved from physical privation, but they have saved themselves from spiritual bigotry.

The Grapes of Wrath is not a period piece about a troublesome past era. The allegory of the Joads applies, for example, to the problems we face today as we strive for a world government. It is an allegory that is applicable wherever prejudice and a sense of self-importance inhibit co-operation, and the message of the book is that co-operation can be achieved only through the willingness of individuals of their own volition to put aside special interests and work towards a common purpose.

The emphasis on individualism and the willing co-operation of individuals explains why the book has been attacked by special interest groups of all kinds. In the course of the narrative, Steinbeck examines and finds fault with four "organized" methods of solving problems: organized charity, organized religion, organized government, organized private enterprise. He rejects two alternatives quickly. Organized charity, symbolized by the Salvation Army, he rejects as distasteful and degrading. At Weedpatch Camp another migrant tells Ma Joad, "Fella tol' us to go to the Salvation Army. . . . We was hungry—they made us crawl for our dinner. They took our dignity. They—I hate 'em. . . . I ain't never seen my man beat before, but them—them Salvation Army done it to 'im" (432). Earlier Tom Joad has questioned the organization's methods. He tells Casy:

> "Las' Christmus in McAlester, Salvation Army come an' done us good. Three solid hours a cornet music, an' we set there. They was bein' nice to us. But if one of us tried to walk out, we'd a-drawed solitary. That's preachin'. Doin' good to a fella that's down an' can't smack ya in the puss for it" (128).

Steinbeck evidently sympathized with Thoreau's statement in *Walden* that "if I knew for a certainty that a man was coming to my house with the conscious design of doing me good, I should run for my life. . . ."

Organized religion with its preoccupation with sin Steinbeck gives equally short shrift. As in most of his other books, he treats the church not with hostility but condescension; perhaps this is why religious organs have criticized his works violently —even institutions that thrive on persecution wince at contempt. The most pious figure in the book is Mrs. Sandry at the Weedpatch Camp, who moans, "They's wicketness in that camp. . . . The poor is tryin' to be rich," and of whom the camp manager says simply, "Try not to hit her. She isn't well. She just isn't well" (437-39). Steinbeck suggests elsewhere in

the novel that religion is a kind of affliction. When Muley
Graves is trying to get Tom to hide from the deputy sheriff
who comes to inspect the deserted Joad farm, he tells Tom,
"You can easy tell yourself you're foolin' them lyin' out like
that. An' it all just amounts to what you tell yourself" (79).

Casy has evidently given up preaching when he has come
to view religion as amounting to what one tells one oneself.
Sin is, as he sees it, a matter of the way one looks at things:
"There ain't no sin and there ain't no virtue. There's just
stuff people do" (32). He expands this view when he later
talks to Uncle John about his wife's death. "For anybody else,"
Casy says, "it was a mistake, but if you think it was a sin—
then it's a sin. A fella builds his own sins right up from the
groun'" (306).

This relativistic view of sin leads Steinbeck into a philosophical mire from which he fails to emerge satisfactorily.
Casy goes on to say, "Some of the things folks do is nice, and
some ain't nice, but that's as far as any man got a right to
say" (32). Who determines, however, what's "nice" and what
isn't? Steinbeck does not, as some critics seem to think, evade
this question completely. As Walter Fuller Taylor points out
in his essay in *Mississippi Quarterly* (Summer, 1959) Steinbeck acknowledges in Chapter Seventeen (265) that certain
"rights" must be respected and others destroyed or else the
little world of the migrant camps "could not exist for even a
night."

Steinbeck never attempts, however, to codify these rights or
to explain how a system for seeing that they are observed will
operate; neither, however, had other transcendentalists, all of
whom seemed to assume that man in his natural state, un-
corrupted by civilized institutions, tended to do the right
thing. What should be emphasized again, however, is that
The Grapes of Wrath is a novel, not a tract—art, not sociology
or philosophy. As an artist Steinbeck is concerned with depicting not prescribing man's behavior. He feels that if people
develop the proper attitude they will be able to govern themselves. He tries to help them see themselves as they are, but
he is not a law-giver.

He does feel that traditional religion no longer enables
man to see himself as he is, that its laws are not applicable

to the situation in which contemporary man finds himself. Steinbeck's attitude is that this religion is all right for those who can afford it, but that in critical times it becomes an unconscionable luxury. This disdainful attitude is suggested by Pa Joad's telling Uncle John, who begins moaning when Tom gets into trouble, "We ain't got the time for your sin now." Ma simply observes, "Uncle John is just a-draggin' along" (535-36). Conventional religious attitudes are clearly represented as hindrances rather than helps in solving the urgent problems of life under unprecedented conditions.

Steinbeck is much more sympathetic toward the government, as is shown by his depiction of the opportunities to recover self-respect offered the migrants at the Weedpatch Camp. "Why ain't they more places like this?" Tom asks (393) and obviously speaks for the author. Yet even though he pictures the camp attractively, Steinbeck does not suggest that the whole burden of solving the problem should or even can be placed upon the government. He never suggests that the migrants should have remained in Oklahoma and sought federal relief, since he is arguing not that the government solve problems but that individuals should learn from experience. The trouble with the Weedpatch Camp is that it provides the migrants with everything but work. The dream of these migrants is not to be supported, but to work land of their own. Steinbeck is definitely no collectivist.

The treatment of organized private enterprise is more complex, since, although Steinbeck criticizes "the ridiculousness of the industrial life" (385) and depicts the companies as "machines and masters" and the employees as "slaves" (43), his objection is primarily that the corporations have become too remote and impersonal and do not "love the land." He definitely advocates private ownership of property. One of the tenant farmers muses, for example:

"Funny thing, how it is. If a man owns a little property, that property is him, it's part of him, and it's like him. . . . Even if he isn't successful, he's big with property. . . . But let a man get property he doesn't see, or can't take time to get his fingers in, or can't be there to walk on it—why then the property is the man . . . he's the servant of his property" (50-51).

Later Casy says in the discussion of a property that is obviously the late William Randolph Hearst's vast San Simeon ranch, "If he needs a million acres to make him feel rich, seems to me he needs it 'cause he feels awful poor inside hisself" (282). In Steinbeck's analysis of "the crime . . . that goes beyond denunciation," he praises the skill of scientists and producers and levels his charges at failures in the system of distributing the product (477). Steinbeck's objection is never to the private enterprise system, but to the irresponsibility of big business. His idea at the time he wrote *The Grapes of Wrath* was that the solution to the nation's ills lay in a system based upon small landholdings.

It is particularly interesting, in view of the attitudes expressed in *The Grapes of Wrath,* to examine an explanation by an American of the modern corporation in one of Steinbeck's latest books, *The Short Reign of Pippin IV.* The son of a California egg-king is talking to a king of France:

". . . here's the funny thing, sir. You take a big corporation in America, say like General Motors or Du Pont or US Steel. The thing they're most afraid of is socialism, and at the same time they themselves are socialist states. . . . Why, if the US Government tried to do one-tenth of what General Motors does, General Motors would go into armed revolt. . . . They don't do it out of kindness, sir. It's just that some of them have found out they can produce and sell more goods that way. They used to fight the employees. That's expensive."

This description of corporations isn't as strange as it sounds from the author of *The Grapes of Wrath.* It should be remembered that in one of the inter-chapters in the novel, Steinbeck tried to explain the significance of the migration and commented, "If you who own things people must have could understand this [growing unity], you might preserve yourself" (206). As some of those not blinded by "fambly" prejudices perceived even at the time of the novel's publication, *The Grapes of Wrath* is not an external attack upon the American economic system, but an internal demand for its reform. Yet Stanley Edgar Hyman is also wrong when he says in his notes on Steinbeck in the *Antioch Review* (June, 1942) that the central message of the novel is an appeal to the class that controls the economy to behave; its main point is that the workers, too, must reform their views if there is to be any real improvement. At bottom, Steinbeck believes, like his great predecessor, Hawthorne, that the only lasting and meaningful reforms originate in the individual human heart.

CHAPTER 10

Steinbeck Goes to War

THE AUTHOR of a best-seller or a critically acclaimed novel is always under pressure, since he faces a crowd of many curious, many expectant, and not a few hostile people asking if he can do it again. When a man has written a novel that is both popularly and critically acclaimed, his position is doubly difficult, especially if he has not made a flash success with a first novel but has climbed laboriously from obscurity to the top of the precarious literary heap.

Steinbeck was in exactly this uncomfortable position after the success of *The Grapes of Wrath*; the reading public clamored for more, asked what would he do next? what was he working on? could he keep it up? His situation was made even less enviable by the outbreak of World War II, which, ironically, largely solved the physical problems depicted in *The Grapes of Wrath* by providing an almost insatiable market in California's mushrooming defense industries for the oversupply of agricultural workers. But not only did the war at least temporarily distract attention from the problems with which Steinbeck had concerned himself for a decade, it also demanded attention as the greatest social catastrophe of a troubled era.

Another novelist might have been free to disregard the war or hold his tongue until favorable trends were apparent. While there was a spate of morale-building fiction and non-fiction about the war effort, the outstanding writers of the thirties were mostly unheard from. Steinbeck, however, had built his reputation on his forthright attack upon social problems of the day; having displayed a predilection for events in the news, he could scarcely ignore the war. But his preoccupation with narrowly defined problems in a particular setting and his absorption in Arthurian lore ill prepared him for dealing with mechanized, global conflict, just as his non-teleological attitudes ill equipped him for stirring up patriotic fervor. The problem of dealing with an international disaster with which he had no first-hand experience with the same perception that he had applied to intra-group struggles he was intimately familiar with was formidable. It is small wonder that Steinbeck's next novel disappointed most readers.

Steinbeck first handled the problem of creating a worthy successor to *The Grapes of Wrath* by trying to avoid it. He spent much of the time between the publication of the novel and the entrance of the United States into World War II in neutral Mexico first on a biological expedition and then in making a movie; but, finally in 1942, he published a novel about the war.

Critics and public were far from agreed about the merits of *The Moon is Down*. A group of distinguished writers, including James Thurber, led the attack on the novel as artificial and soft toward the Nazis. Steinbeck attracted supporters among less emotional readers, but not even his champions could claim that the new book compared with its predecessor. Now that the heat of war-engendered tensions has died down, the general opinion is that the book is a failure both as propaganda and fiction. It has been most popular among European liberals, who are willing to overlook its defects because of appreciation of the liberty-loving spirit that inspired it. American critics, however, more impressed by achievement than intention, give the novel scant notice.

Their attitude is justified. Even though written like *Of Mice and Men* for almost direct dramatization, *The Moon is Down* lacks the sense of almost overpoweringly urgent movement towards an irresistible catastrophe that distinguished the earlier narrative. One is aware of one magnificent character, Mayor Orden, who grows in stature and moves splendidly towards an unworthy doom; but the author too rarely focuses upon the Mayor. Steinbeck tried here, as in *The Forgotten Village*, the method of depicting a widespread situation by centering upon one small village, but the specific location is too ill-defined for Steinbeck's personalized method to work well, and at least one major figure is not completely enough characterized for his motives to be comprehensible. One feels too often—as James Thurber complained of the play version—that the characters have walked in not from the streets of a village but from their theatre dressing rooms.

A principal reason for the artificiality of the novel is that Steinbeck got himself into the same predicament that Coleridge did in "The Rime of the Ancient Mariner"; he failed to correlate his moral with his plot; or, to use some useful terms from I. A. Richards' critical theory, the vehicle (the "narrative" through which a thesis is metaphorically presented) and the tenor (the thesis) fail to go together. The moral is exemplary and the story moving, but the two fail to reinforce each other as they must in a satisfying allegory. The ostensible message of the novel is embodied in Mayor Orden's statement to the leader of the invading party near the end of the book as the mayor is about to be executed as a hostage:

> "The people don't like to be conquered, sir, and so they will not be. Free men cannot start a war, but once it is started, they can fight on in defeat. Herd men, followers of a leader, cannot do that, and so it is always the herd men who win battles and the free men who win wars. You will find that is so, sir."

Indeed, events proved it so. Surely no one on the Allied side could condemn this heartening oration. Unfortunately it remains oratory; the story does not illustrate its truth.

It is impossible and probably irrelevant to ascertain what caused Steinbeck to fail, although part of his trouble may have been overconfidence. Lisca reports that the novelist was already convinced that the fascists had lost the war when he wrote the novel, but his optimism was not generally shared. Against the background of the time at which it appeared, *The Moon is Down* was—and still may be—read as another tragedy of the Socratic spirit. "The debt shall be paid," a doctor tells the Mayor, who is about to be executed; Steinbeck evidently intended this as an assertion, but most people would have read it as an expression of pious hope. Nothing short of the destruction of a German detachment in a Commando raid could have provided a microcosmic vision of victory in troubled times. Steinbeck would probably have considered such a device too "slick" (although a few years later in *Sweet Thursday* he was to use worse).

It is impossible now, however, to re-create emotions felt at the height of the war. What we can analyze is what message the situation Steinbeck deals with could have illustrated. Some critics have complained that Steinbeck treats the invaders too impartially—does not become angry enough with them—but this objection could be answered with the statement in *In Dubious Battle* that the other side is made up of men, too. Lisca points out in his discussion of the German Colonel Lanser what is really wrong with the extended treatment of the invaders: "After reading the first description of him one knows as much about him as one does at the end of the book." In neither the invaders nor the conquered people do we witness the kind of growth that occurs in the Joads.

The least convincing character is, however, neither the stereotyped invaders nor their philosophical victims, but Mr. Corell, "popular storekeeper" and local quisling, who betrays the community to the invaders. The reader simply is not told enough about him to be able to understand his behavior. The first problem is where he came from. His conversations with Colonel Lanser suggest that he is a native of the occupying power.[1] If he is an invader, however, he must have been planted in the village long ago to have insinuated himself so firmly into the graces of the citizens; for, as *In Dubious Battle* and *The Forgotten Village* indicate, it takes a long time for strangers to overcome the suspicions of a small community. The natives of Steinbeck's seaport may be either unusually affable or simple-minded, but in either case their town would be a poor microcosm. If Corell is a native of the invaded nation and not one of the "herd men," Steinbeck would need to explain—as he doesn't—why the local love of liberty hasn't affected him.

The novel would be more credible if Corell was, as many quislings were, a native of the occupied country who sold out in hopes of gaining personal power, settling grudges against his neighbors, and otherwise advancing private causes. If Corell was such a person, however, Steinbeck's thesis that the struggle is between "free men" and "herd men" would be contradicted, since Corell would be not an exemplar but an exploiter of "herd men." Just exactly what Corell's position is, even as an agent of the invader, is far from clear. When he first speaks of his treachery he announces: "I work for what I believe in. That is an honorable thing." A little later, however, told that his work in the village is done, he argues that he has made a place for himself there and belongs there.[2] When we last see him demanding Mayor Orden's execution, we learn that he has actually gone over Colonel Lanser's head to get his own way. A good herd man would not circumvent channels.

The struggle depicted in the novel is actually not between "herd men" and "free men" at all—we never even really see any "herd men," only their exploiters. Even Colonel Lanser's behavior is incomprehensible unless he has a lust for power that he hoped—against the evidence of his own experience— he might achieve through aiding the Nazis. It is the failure of the invaders in the book to be the kind of "herd men" that the author says they are that has disturbed readers.

The struggle in this novel, like that in *In Dubious Battle,* is really between two attitudes toward the mass of the people, as they are reflected in two techniques of leadership. Mayor Orden, whom even Colonel Lanser describes as knowing what the people are "doing, thinking, without asking, because he will think what they think," represents the kind of leader, like Doctor Burton, who honors human dignity and takes his cues from the people. The Colonel, who tells the Mayor, "The people have no say," represents the other—the kind toward whom Socrates directed his famous reproach, "If you think that by killing men, you can prevent someone from censuring your evil lives, you are mistaken."

Steinbeck, however, fails to come to grips in this novel with the problem that he tackled in *In Dubious Battle.* The invaders here are carbon copies of the agitators (and the growers) in the strike novel. They are perhaps even more alike than Steinbeck would have wished to acknowledge, since admitting the similarity would have entailed admitting also that the invader's agents (like the labor agitators) were able to gain power by exciting the grievances of discontented people who felt themselves misused. What one of the conquered people needs to say to Corell or Lanser in *The Moon is Down,* but never does, is a variation on what Jim says to Mac near the end of *In Dubious Battle*: "Sometimes I get the feeling that you're persecuting me not for the party, but for yourself."

One gets the feeling that Corell and Lanser are on the invader's side not because they believe in the Cause but because they seek to profit from it personally. Corell has apparently insinuated himself into the villagers' favor by using the same kind of Madison Avenue techniques that Mac uses to win over the workmen's leaders, and both show the same basic contempt for the common man. Thus the moral of the book is not that although free people become soft, they fight back when oppressed; but rather that although people are not sufficiently suspicious of flattery, they become enraged when they learn they have been bilked. Actually the book warns—like most of Steinbeck's—against becoming complacent and making precipitate judgments of "good" and "bad" without looking at "the whole thing."

Apparently, however, the author had become too complacent himself. A real weakness of Steinbeck's position is not that he is insufficiently critical of the Nazis, but that he is insufficiently respectful of their resources and shows them driven to desperate measures in an unrealistic hurry. Looking back, it is difficult to gainsay Steinbeck, for his optimism was justified, but could spirit alone have won for the Allies without the assistance of superior force? Everything did not work out so smoothly as Steinbeck would have it in his famous phrase about "the flies conquering the flypaper." He leaves no room for such developments as V-rockets and atomic bombs.

It is hard to believe, too, that the opposing forces were as neatly divided into herd and free men as Steinbeck would have us believe. Steinbeck, who earlier wrote a warning that using labels like *good* and *bad* may cause one to lose one's inspection license, freely applies these labels himself in this novel. True, he indicates doubts in one place when he has Mayor Orden say, in response to a suggestion that in England there still may be "men in power who do not dare put weapons in the hands of the common people": "If such people govern England and America, the world is lost, anyway." Presumably, since the British do send the suggested weapons to the common people, doubts on this score are dispelled.

What Steinbeck refuses to face here, however, is the fact that choosing sides is often not a matter of choosing good over evil, but choosing the lesser of evils. He had suggested in *In Dubious Battle* that only non-commitment is really admirable, but he probably found that in the face of war he could not maintain the "curse on both your houses" attitude that fellow-Californian Robinson Jeffers did. If he had written a war novel consistent with *In Dubious Battle*, of course, it would have provoked a reaction that would have made the quarrel over *The Moon is Down* insignificant. Steinbeck may have been too completely committed to the Allied cause to remain rigidly objective in discussing the war; but he may also simply not have wished to risk antagonizing the public in the way he would with an austerely objective novel.

In either case, *The Moon is Down* demonstrates that he was not able to face the problem of the individual lust for power as was, for example, Joyce Cary in some of his novels. Peter Lisca reports that Steinbeck "was too disheartened by what he had seen of the war to prolong the experience in any way" and decided not to publish a novel based on his observations after returning from the war zone in 1943. I suspect that what this means is that Steinbeck had found that there were some aspects of human behavior that he, like the scientist in "The Snake," could not face without becoming "afraid" and "sick."

Instead of facing the problems that writing about the war raised, Steinbeck turned to writing *Cannery Row*, a book about a subject seemingly remote from the war in which he at last delineated his concept of the modern "hero." This hero, however, lived in a world where battles were fought with brains, not guns. I suspect that what had most dismayed Steinbeck about the war was his horrified glimpse of the amount of infantilism abroad in a world that could resort to mass bloodshed in its drive for power. A powerful war novel could be written by depicting men like Pepe in Steinbeck's "Flight" being manipulated by those like Mac in *In Dubious Battle,* but Steinbeck probably simply did not want to think about the implications of such relationships on such a scale.

CHAPTER 11

The Intricate Music of Cannery Row

STEINBECK told Peter Lisca that *Cannery Row* was written as a relaxation from the depression he suffered because of the war. The remoteness of the book from the pressing issues of the day indicates that it is certainly a kind of "escapist" literature, but it would be a ludicrous mistake to confuse this subtly ironic book with the tons of escapist fiction tailored to the formulas of the slick magazines and designed to take readers' minds off their own failures and frustrations by assuring them that there is a land where virtue as conventionally defined is inevitably rewarded and the virtues really and truly do live happily ever after.

Rather than a comforting confection, *Cannery Row,* which its author called a "poisoned cream puff," is another letter of advice to an erring world; but, as had happened before, the advice went not only unheeded but unperceived. After this, Steinbeck was to strain to make his points clear to the reader; and as he belabored his points, the quality of his fiction suffered. Unless Steinbeck shows great improvement, *Cannery Row* is his last distinguished work of art. Quite appropriately, it both sums up the charges he had leveled at society in his earlier novels and for the first time shows how the individual may not only strive for but achieve a measure of contentment in a generally depraved society.

The enemy Steinbeck attacks—the destructive force that preys on the world—is, as usual in his novels, respectability: the desire to attain an unnatural security for one's self by ruthlessly disregarding the feelings of others. Not, however, since *The Pastures of Heaven* and "The White Quail," had the forces of respectability been subjected to such a sus-

tained attack. The ironical contrast Steinbeck seeks to emphasize in all his fiction is summed up by Doc, the central figure
in *Cannery Row,* when he tells a caller:

> "It has always seemed strange to me. . . . The things we
> admire in men, kindness and generosity, openness, honesty,
> understanding and feeling are the concomitants of failure
> in our system. And those traits we detest, sharpness, greed,
> acquisitiveness, meanness, egotism and self-interest are the
> traits of success. And while men admire the quality of the first
> they love the produce of the second."

Man then, as Steinbeck sees him—and as his political behavior surely testifies—is a curiously divided animal, who
professes admiration for one thing and demonstrates affection
for another. Steinbeck further sees this division between what
man says and does as responsible for his frustrations and con-
flicts. These points are hardly unique; many others have made
them—Christ and Socrates, for example. The lesson, however,
must be continually retaught since it remains unlearned.
Steinbeck, despite the misgivings expressed in *In Dubious
Battle* and *Of Mice and Men,* retained some lingering faith
that the lesson might be learned. He had experimented with
teaching it negatively through the deft use of bitter satire in
Cup of Gold, The Pastures of Heaven, "St. Katy, the Virgin,"
the inter-chapters in *The Grapes of Wrath,* and positively
through a sympathetic depiction of an individual's education
into full humanity in *The Red Pony* and the Joad story in
The Grapes of Wrath.

In *Cannery Row* he tries once more a combined method.
Although the novel has been one of the author's most popular
works and has been hailed as a classic of American humor, it
has not, I believe, been received as the author hoped. He has
complained that the design of the book has been overlooked,
and it has not yet been recognized that *Cannery Row,* far from
being a loosely related collection of diverting episodes, is
actually one of the most intricately and artfully constructed
and most witheringly critical of novels.

Even the structure of the book has proved disconcerting
since it has no "plot" in the usual sense of the word. Just how
the attempts of certain denizens of Cannery Row in Monterey,

California, to honor Doc, proprietor of Western Biological Laboratory, with a party provides an organic framework for the novel has been overlooked because the main story does not follow the conventional plot line of slowly rising and rapidly falling action but is periodically interrupted, as in *The Grapes of Wrath*, by inter-chapters that comment upon the action.

The chapters carrying forward the main narrative (the odd-numbered ones from 1 to 17, Chapters 18, 20, 21, 23, 25, 27, 29, 30 and possibly 32), which describe the development of the idea of a party for Doc, the first unsuccessful party and its disheartening aftermath, the rekindling of spirit and the successful second party, actually follow (as is most fitting in a novel set on a seacoast) the pattern of a wave, growing slowly, hitting a reef or barrier, dividing and crashing prematurely, re-forming, rising to a great height and crashing at last on the beach itself. The structure might also be considered as analogous to the efforts of a spider to build a web in an especially challenging location, who at first fails but at last succeeds in throwing a frail thread across a formidable space. Both of these parallels are, of course, drawn from nature and describe kinds of natural rhythms. Steinbeck seems to have made an effort to employ some such "natural" rather than a conventionally artistic structure as the novel's framework.

Once discerned, the pattern is easy to trace in detail. There is only a hint of a wave forming on the tranquil surface of life on Cannery Row when at the end of the first chapter, Mack and the boys at the Palace Flophouse and Grill observe, "That Doc is a fine fellow. We ought to do something for him." By the end of Chapter 5, the boys' sentiment is generally shared: "Everyone who thought of [Doc] thought next, 'I really must do something nice for [him]." This "something nice," however is, like the Palace Flophouse itself, "no sudden development." In Chapter 7, the desire to do something has crystallized into the desire to give a party for Doc. In Chapter 9, the boys decide to raise money for this party by hunting frogs; and chapters 11, 13 and 15 follow the movements of the frog-hunt through their none-too-smooth course.

Between chapters 16 and 21, the design of the novel is flawed; Lisca reports that the publishers dropped one inter-chapter from the novel and I suspect that it was from this section. Enough of the design remains, however, to make it appear that the "wave" divides at this point and that in chapters 17 and 18 we follow Doc, whom the partly will supposedly honor, out of town on a collecting expedition, while in chapters 20 and 21, we attend the party that the guest of honor misses which results in the devastation of his laboratory.

In Chapter 23, the wave, temporarily divided and smashed, reassembles and we are pushed rapidly forward toward the triumphant end of the novel. The recovery of Mack-and-the-boys' dog, Darling, from distemper symbolizes a general lifting of the pall that has hung over Cannery Row; and when Dora, the Madame of the Bear Flag Restaurant, suggests that Mack repair the damage that the unsuccessful party caused by giving a party that Doc gets to, the temporarily dissipated energies of the community are refocused.

Preparations are laid for the party and gather momentum in chapters 25 and 27, while in chapters 29 and 30, with a tremendous crescendo the party itself occurs, ending with an explosive flourish as a twenty-five-foot string of firecrackers is lit. In Chapter 32, the wave crashed and spent, we find Doc alone clearing up in its wake and reading, as he has at the party, from the Sanskrit lyric, "Black Marigolds." This conclusion, like those of *Cup of Gold* and *The Grapes of Wrath*, has invited speculation since the narrative itself obviously ends when Doc finishes cleaning up after the party, wipes his hands, and turns off the record player. Something beyond the ending of the story is clearly added in the last page of the novel. To see what it is, however, we must first examine the inter-chapters.

These are probably even more disturbing to the reader with stereotyped expectations than those in *The Grapes of Wrath*. While a few in the earlier novel were included for argumentative purposes, most were obviously designed to universalize the story of the Joads. Some of the inter-chapters in *Cannery Row* are also very obviously related to the central narrative; but, since some employ the same characters, it is not, as Lisca points out, always easy to tell which are inter-chapters.

The only real problem, however, is posed by chapters 10

and 28 (both concerning Doc's relation to the spastic Frankie) and even these could be omitted without damaging the structure of the main narrative. Their relationship to the rest of the novel becomes apparent only in view of the final part of the last chapter. A different kind of problem is posed by six chapters (12, 14, 19, 24, 26 and 31) which do not even concern or universalize characters in the main narrative and which seem merely interpolated fables. Even Lisca seems to feel that, if there is any really systematic patterning throughout the book, "it escapes detection."

I believe, however, that a closer correlation than has been noticed can be found between the chapters of the main narrative and the inter-chapters and that it can also be demonstrated that each inter-chapter is intended, like many of those in *The Grapes of Wrath*, to universalize the implications of the chapter in the main narrative that it follows. "Associated" would perhaps be the best word to use to describe the paired chapters since they usually reinforce each other in making some single point.

The clue to the purpose of the inter-chapters is found in Chapter 2, the first of them, in which Steinbeck writes: "The word is a symbol." "The Word," he continues, commenting on characters introduced in the first chapter, "sucks up Cannery Row, digests it and spews it out. . . . Lee Chong is more than a Chinese grocer. He must be. Perhaps he is evil balanced and held suspended by good. . . ." The purpose of this comment, as of the next in which Mack and the boys are described as "the Virtues, the Graces, the Beauties of the hurried mangled craziness of Monterey and the cosmic Monterey," is to drive home to the reader that this is not merely an arch narrative about a group of unique specimens, but an allegory—that these characters are not only themselves in Monterey, but symbols of universal tendencies in the world that this setting microcosmically represents. Certainly if any author has ever given us license to read his novel as an allegory and to search for symbolic inter-relationships between the one long and many short narratives included, Steinbeck has here. One misses the point of Chapter 2 by regarding it as simply a sentimental attempt to beatify the boys at the Palace Flophouse.

In chapters 3 and 4, the note of tragedy that is to increase in intensity and then to be gradually tempered is struck. Those who carry away the impression that *Cannery Row* is a humorous book do so on the overpowering strength of the description of the parties toward the end of the book; one who stopped reading with the fourth chapter could hardly fail to find the novel profoundly depressing. The third chapter introduces Dora and the noble prostitutes of the Bear Flag Restaurant, but is devoted principally to the story of William, the establishment's former bouncer, who commits suicide when the tight society of Cannery Row rejects him and laughs at him.

The fourth chapter is a cryptic account of an old Chinaman who daily makes his mysterious way through the Row; most people fear him, but one brave boy makes fun of him and is rewarded with a vision that makes him whimper. The old man means various things to different people, but he seems actually to symbolize through his utter detachment from the world around him, the thing people fear most—to very old people, this is death; but, to young boys like the one who makes fun of him, it is loneliness. The old Chinaman symbolizes the terrors of isolation to the person who must rely upon the opinion of the world around him, rather than upon his internal resources, for happiness.

These chapters are related in two ways. Both are "essays in loneliness"—as Ed Ricketts, Steinbeck's good friend and the model for Doc in the novel, said *Cannery Row* was as a whole. Both concern people who have either the experience or the vision of being cut off from the rest of the world. They are more specifically tied together by the motivations of the principal characters in them. William, the bouncer in Chapter 3, finally commits suicide because he realizes that, when he finally impresses someone that this is his intent "he had to do it," even though it then seemed silly. Similarly, Andy, the boy in the next chapter, taunts the old Chinaman "to keep his self-respect." Both incidents illustrate that a person may be driven to uncomfortable, frightening, and even suicidal lengths to keep up a front. Even if Steinbeck was not writing directly about the war in *Cannery Row*, he was commenting on it obliquely.

The next two chapters introduce Doc. The relationship between them is different from that of the previous pair. Chapter 5 generalizes about Doc, and Chapter 6 demonstrates his characteristics in specific situations. The main point in Chapter 5 is that Doc's "mind had no horizon—and his sympathy had no warp." In the next chapter this lack of horizon and bias—as well as the contrast between Doc and the more limited characters in the novel—is demonstrated when he tells Hazel, one of Mack's gang, that he thinks stink-bugs keep their tails up in the air because they are praying. "If we did something as inexplicable and strange, we'd probably be praying," he continues. "Let's get the hell out of here," is the only reply from the good-natured but simple-minded man unable to cope with analogical thinking or shockingly unprecedented ideas.

The attack on respectability begins on a muted note in the next pair of chapters. In Chapter 7, we learn that Mack and the boys have their own code of behavior. When it is suggested that they go to work in a cannery to earn a few dollars to give a party for Doc, Mack rejects the idea. "We got good reputations and we don't want to spoil them," he explains. "Every one of us keeps a job for a month or more when we take one. That's why we can always get a job when we need one." Steinbeck makes the point that even these "bums" have respectable standards, but they are the masters and not the slaves of them.

In the droll eighth chapter, we see the opposite side of the coin. When Mr. Sam Malloy becomes a "landlord" renting out large pipes as sleeping rooms, his wife is overwhelmed with a desire for respectability, which finally asserts itself as a desire for curtains although there are no windows in the old boiler that is the Malloy home. When her husband tells her that he does not "begrutch" her the curtains, but that they simply have no use for them, she sobs: "Men just don't understand how a woman feels." Her standards are her master. Although seemingly only an amusing sketch, the chapter contains the germ of Steinbeck's argument against respectability as the enslaver of persons.

In the next two chapters Doc is further characterized. It becomes apparent that although his mind has no horizons, nature has placed physical limitations upon him as upon all men. We learn also that he is not a sentimental optimist: he has no illusions about people. He is suspicious of Mack, for he has been victimized before by schemes like the proposed trip to gather turtles; he even says, when asked if the bite of false teeth is poisonous: "I guess everything that comes out of the human mouth is poison." He is also like all men: powerless in the face of nature's mistakes.

In one of the most moving chapters of the novel, the tenth, Steinbeck recapitulates the story of George and Lennie in *Of Mice and Men* in his portrayal of the relationship between Doc and Frankie. Frankie, like Lennie, is one of nature's anomalies; he is unable to learn and there is "something a little wrong with his co-ordination." Doc shows the boy the first affection he has known and does all in his power to aid him; but, when Frankie's co-ordination fails, there is nothing that can be done. Doc is completely defeated in his efforts just as Franklin Gomez in *The Pastures of Heaven* had been in his to help Tularecito. Steinbeck stresses here, as elsewhere, the impossibility of the human quest for perfection; man is helpless in the face of nature's imperfections. It is misleading, even metaphorically, to view Doc as a kind of neighborhood god. He is better regarded as striving to be what Steinbeck respects as the best imperfect man can hope to be in an imperfect universe.

In the next pair of chapters, the tempo of the novel accelerates as Steinbeck once more levels his artillery at his prime target—respectability. The twelfth chapter—the wry tale of the respectable citizens' insistence that the discarded insides of the famous humorist Josh Billings be given the same respectable burial as his preserved carcass—is a savage burlesque on the ignorance and literalism of the respectable. The chapter does not at first, however, appear connected with the preceding chapter about the Palace Flophouse boys' difficulty fixing the truck they have borrowed for the frog hunt; it seems merely an amusing reinforcement of one of the book's general points.

The two chapters are closely related, however, by a brief passage in each. Both burlesque respectable people's suspicion of innovations that inevitably change their lives. The eleventh chapter contains Steinbeck's comment that as a result of the Model T Ford "the theory of the Anglo-Saxon home became so warped that it never quite recovered." The twelfth chapter notes the resistance to the embalming of bodies when the practice was first introduced on the grounds that "it was sacrilegious since there was no provision for it in any sacred volume." These points made, Steinbeck again contrasts the boys with the respectable citizenry to the detriment of the latter, calling Gay, the mechanic with a special gift for the creatures of progress, "the little mechanic of God, the St. Francis of all things that turn and twist and explode," while poking fun at the "stern men" who oblige the embalmer to retrieve Josh Billings' tripas and "wash them reverently."

The connection between the next two chapters is more immediately apparent. Just as the ninth and tenth chapters have recapitulated the theme of *Of Mice and Men,* the thirteenth and fourteenth present in capsule form the theme of *Tortilla Flat*: possession of property takes the fun out of life. In Chapter 13, we are introduced to the owner of the land upon which Mack and the boys trespass during the frog hunt. "The land's posted," he yells at them impatiently, almost hysterically; "No fishing, hunting, fires, camping. Now you just pack up and put that fire out and get off this land." Mack's solicitous attentions to the man's dog, however, eventually mellow him; but the point Steinbeck is driving at is brought home at the end of the chapter when Hazel observes that Mack could have been President if he'd wished. So what? asks another in effect, "There wouldn't be no fun in that." The owner of the land has been having no fun; nor has the watchman of the private beach of Hopkins Marine Station, where the action of the brief fourteenth chapter occurs. When he yells at some soldiers and their girls, "You got to get off. This is private property!" one of the soldiers simply replies, "Why don't you take a flying fuggut the moon." One of Steinbeck's perennial arguments is that obsession with property destroys joy and human sympathy.

The fifteenth and sixteenth chapters present another contrast, this time between two types of women. In the fifteenth chapter Mack and the boys visit the owner of the land and discover that his wife, a paragon of respectability, has been elected to the Assembly for the district and is off making speeches when the legislature isn't in session. In thus serving the public by promoting herself, she ignores her domestic duties. In one of the most malicious passages in the novel, Steinbeck characterizes her type:

> The kind of women who put papers on shelves and had little towels . . . instinctively distrusted and disliked Mack and the boys. Such women knew that they were the worst threats to a home, for they offered ease and thought and companionship as opposed to neatness, order, and properness.

Chapter 16 presents a contrasting picture of Dora, the Madame of the Bear Flag Restaurant, who takes over the responsibility for the care of the whole community during an influenza epidemic, despite the fact that it comes at a bad time for her own business. Together, the two chapters, one of the most effective pairs in the novel, present a telling contrast between selfish respectability and unselfish disreputability. Steinbeck's point is missed, however, if his attitude is construed as praise of prostitution; he is simply using the prostitutes to emphasize his scorn of thoughtless respectability and to condemn the making of judgments on the basis of superficial categories.

The next six chapters present something of an organizational problem. As the book stands it is most satisfactory to read chapters 17 and 18 as a single narrative, Chapter 19 as the commenting inter-chapter, chapters 20 and 21 as another continuous narrative, and Chapter 22 as the summarizing inter-chapter. My guess, however, is that the omitted inter-chapter—later published separately as "The Time the Wolves Ate the Vice-Principal"—should follow the present Chapter 18 and that the present Chapter 19 should be placed between 17 and 18.

Chapters 17 and 18 are the only two in which the action moves away from the Monterey region, for we follow Doc on a collecting trip to La Jolla. The change of scene is not necessitated by the theme of the story but by the plot which requires getting Doc out of town during the first party. Chapter 17 is principally about Doc's love of truth, his discovery that it is not "a general love," and his resorting to subterfuge to protect his privacy because people are unable to communicate honestly with each other without becoming suspicious. An inter-chapter seems necessary after this chapter, but we plunge instead directly into the eighteenth chapter, an account of Doc's discovery at La Jolla during low tide of the body of a dead girl in an underwater rock crevice.

The present Chapter 19 may belong after the present Chapter 17 because the flag-pole incident discussed in detail in 19 is mentioned in 17 and both comment bitterly on people's morbid curiosity. Chapter 17 points out that people trust those who do what will make money but distrust those who do what they like to do. Chapter 19 shows the profit motive at work as curiosity about the flag-pole skater increases department store sales, and also indicates the kind of ugly question that people long to ask those who may find artistic satisfaction in the performance of a difficult feat—even if it is only flag-pole skating.

The present Chapter 18 develops further the point about people's depraved curiosity. When Doc tells an inhabitant of the region about the dead girl, all that the latter wishes to know is whether the body was "rotten or eat up?" Although this man has lived in this region all his life he has never known that octopi are there, because, as Doc tells him, "You've got to look for them"—and he is obviously not the intellectually curious type. There have been few such portraits of malignant, greedy ignorance even in Steinbeck's work since *The Pastures of Heaven.*

The attack on money-madness and insensitivity that has been building up through all three of these chapters is climaxed in the omitted inter-chapter, "The Time the Wolves Ate the Vice-Principal." Since this is one of Steinbeck's most gruesome works, I am inclined to think that the publishers omitted it from the novel not because it seemed irrelevant, but because they thought it would be too grisly for American readers who like to hear about death only when it is treated sadistically. The chapter, a masterpiece of objective naturalism, tells of the gathering of a pack of wolves on the Salinas court-house lawn, their ranging about the town, and their eating the ailing vice-principal of the local high school on the steps of the house of a woman who sleeps through the whole incident.

Like Chapter 18, it emphasizes people's ignorance of what is happening right on their doorsteps. The idea that the wolves range while the town sleeps also has implications that extend far beyond Salinas and relate to the general themes of the novel. Steinbeck here makes one of his most memorable comments on the complacent attitude that facilitated the development of conditions resulting in the War. One wonders, furthermore, if there is not some particular significance in the fact that the wolves gather on the court-house lawn and destroy an educator. Whether there is a specific attack on political anti-intellectualism here or not, the chapter is definitely not irrelevant and should have been included in the book; for, in a sense, it is the capstone of Steinbeck's attack on the average person's insensitivity to and distrust of the truth.

Chapters 20 and 21 are really one long description of the failure of the first party for Doc. This catastrophic affair, which the guest of honor misses and which greatly damages his laboratory, casts a pall over Cannery Row. We get the first indication that its inhabitants have not led lives of unrelieved joy when Mack, dipping back into his past for the only time in the novel, reveals that he has been haunted by failure and that his life on Cannery Row is not so much a triumph of uninhibited individualism as an acknowledgment of and resignation to his inadequacies. "Ever'thing I done turned sour," he tells Doc, explaining that he was once married;

"If I done a good thing it got poisoned up some way. If I give her a present they was something wrong with it. She only got hurt from me. . . . Same thing ever' place 'til I just got to clowning. I don't do nothin' but clown no more. Try to make the boys laugh."

There is a dark side to the Bohemian life; its joys are intense but short-lived. Exactly the same point is made in Chapter 22 about Henri, the painter who devotes his life to building a boat he does not wish to finish. Like Mack, Henri has enjoyed many successes; many women have shared his boat with him. But "all of these young women had left him for the same reason . . . they definitely felt the need of a toilet." One cannot, Steinbeck suggests in these two chapters, enjoy anything more than short-lived successes alternating with disappointments unless one makes some concessions to civilization.

Chapters 23 and 24 concern the turning of defeat into victory. Like the two preceding, they repeat a point in order to drive it home. The message seems to be that a person's confidence can be restored by his having a sense of successfully doing something useful. In Chapter 23, Mack and the boys, crushed by the failure of the party, have their spirits restored when the grave illness of the dog Darling at last gives them "something to do" and their ministrations restore the pup to health. Similarly in Chapter 24, when Tom Talbot's situation seems hopeless and his wife Mary's seemingly irrepressible good spirits fail to rouse him, his taking over when she is incapable of dealing with a cat which is destroying a mouse removes the lines from his forehead. The two episodes emphasize once more the general idea underlying the whole book that satisfaction comes from unselfishly helping others rather than from promoting one's own interests.

In the next pair of chapters, Steinbeck abruptly changes his technique and writes not of reinforcing but contrasting incidents, like those in chapters 11 and 12. Both chapters 25 and 26 deal with human resourcefulness in satisfying not physical but psychical wants. In the twenty-fifth chapter we see this resourcefulness being used constructively when Mack devises and executes an elaborate scheme to find out Doc's birth date without giving away the idea that a birthday party is being planned. In the twenty-sixth chapter, on the other hand, the cheerfulness of the last few chapters is dispelled by the bitter picture of the way in which an ingenious but bored boy cruelly baits the weaker son of a suicide victim in order to create some "excitement" for himself. The viciousness of undisciplined physical and intellectual strength has rarely been as bitterly condemned as in this brief and almost entirely conversational interlude, which also powerfully makes the point that Steinbeck had stressed as early as *Cup of Gold*: those who think it is a pleasure to be a child have forgotten their own childhoods.

Matters are by this time moving rapidly towards a climax.

The next two chapters, like the ninth and tenth, serve as a reminder that there are limits to the ability of even the most able. They also diffuse the black-and-white contrast made in the preceding pair of chapters by showing that love does not, after all, always bring joy and that pain does not result only from spite. Both chapters 27 and 28 show how we may suffer because of those we love. Doc, learning of the plans for the party in his honor, feels "great warmth," but also "quakes inwardly" because "he knew he would have trouble at the bank the first of the month. Three or four such parties, he thought, and he would surely lose the laboratory." His trouble is not only, however, that his friends' affection costs him money; he suffers a more dispiriting difficulty when Frankie, learning of the party, steals a clock to give Doc. When told that "the doctor thinks we better put [Frankie] away," Doc realizes that the situation is hopeless. On the eve of the party to honor him, he suffers one of his most affecting losses. Here Steinbeck makes the point that he would have to make if he had written a really significant war novel: even over the moment of victory hangs the shadow of defeat.

The pattern of the novel changes slightly at the end, for an inter-chapter precedes the chapter with which it is paired so that the book may end on the affirmative note Steinbeck wishes finally to strike. Before this pair of chapters, we have been carried in chapters 29 and 30 with breath-taking rapidity through the events of the day of the party itself. Having come to the climax of his tale, Steinbeck dispenses with the allegory—except for making brief preparation for the last chapter by having Doc read from the Sanskrit poem "Black Marigolds." He is intent here simply on describing the delightful air of anticipation and the subsequent overflow of spirits when people settle down at last to having a good time. It would be impertinent to interrupt this saturnalia with an interpolated tale, however edifying.

If *Cannery Row* were, however, simply an escapist novel about the outrageous actions of a bunch of jovial pariahs, it would end with the fireworks that bring down the curtain on the party—not with a whimper, but a bang. It actually ends with neither. After the party is over, there are two more chapters, and it is these that lift the novel out of the realm of diverting local color stories to place it among those that make a profound comment on the uniqueness of the human condition.

A much greater relationship exists between the last two chapters of this novel than is at first evident. Their full significance can be appreciated only when they are read together. The next-to-last chapter about a gopher who finds a secure home but no mate and who is obliged to move back into dangerous territory in order to find female company is obviously a wry commentary on the difficulty of attaining both security and affection. Its meaning is not, however, so obvious as it seems; and the chapter may be misread if it is taken as the same kind of "beast fable" as the allegory of the land turtle (Chapter 3) in *The Grapes of Wrath,* which it superficially resembles.

Steinbeck has sometimes been condemned for treating men as if they were no different from other animals; but exactly what he is attempting to do in the last two chapters of *Cannery Row* is to distinguish men from the other animals— or at least to indicate that men have capabilities available to no other animals, if they will but avail themselves of them. The gopher chapter, the thirty-first, is not an allegorical comment upon man like the turtle episode in the earlier novel; the gopher here is a gopher; and the point of the chapter is that the creature that lives merely by physical sensations must sacrifice security to the satisfaction of its physical desires. If Steinbeck thought, however, that this principle necessarily applied to all men, the book would have ended with this chapter—or would probably never have been written at all.

The last chapter has a much less obvious meaning; it is one of Steinbeck's most cryptic. Comparison with the preceding chapter, however, suggests an interpretation. In the final chapter, after Doc finishes cleaning up, he reads aloud to himself from the Sanskrit poem "Black Marigolds," a section concluding with a verse that begins: "Even now / I know that I have savored the hot taste of life. . . ." Meanwhile "white rats scampered and scrambled in their cages" and rattlesnakes "lay still and stared into space with their dusty frowning eyes."

The point of this final contrast is that man is not like these animals; he is different because he has the unique ability, celebrated in the poem, to preserve, recollect, and even re-create his experiences. It is not necessary for him to live day-by-day like the other animals or to forfeit security for physical affection like the gopher. Once he has "savored the hot taste of life," the recollection remains. Even if he has had an experience "just for a small and forgotten time," like the speaker in the poem, he can live on the strength of his memories. And the strongest of these memories are those that are preserved in works of art. "Black Marigolds" is introduced in the last chapters of *Cannery Row* not only because of what it says but because of what it is: a symbol of man's highest achievement. Ultimately this novel is about the man who has learned with the assistance of art to triumph over his immediate situation and surroundings.

William, the bouncer in Chapter 3, is the man who is like the gopher: the man without other resources, who, deprived of human affection, must destroy himself. Doc is the man who survives, the heroic figure. Doc is not perfect; he is not infallible. He loses his head, and he is defeated—as Jody in *The Red Pony* learned man is defeated—by death, by the imperfections of nature, and by the shortcomings of his friends. Doc is a man who has learned that love brings suffering, but he is one who has learned to find compensation for the frailties of human nature and other aspects of physical nature in what Yeats called "monuments of unaging intellect." He is one of those few "wisest," whom Pater celebrated, who spend their mortal interval "in art and song."

Cannery Row then is not even simply an attack upon conventional respectability and an inflated sense of self-importance, although Steinbeck sees these twin evils as the truly destructive forces in a sick world. The novel is rather a defense of the creative spirit, a defense of poetry. It is Steinbeck's answer to the challenge of the war—not a novel about the physical battle against a transient enemy to make life possible, but one about the intellectual struggle against the enduring enemy to make life worthwhile.

It is no wonder that the pages of the novel, like the nights in Cannery Row, are filled with the music from Doc's phonograph; the book celebrates man's music-making skill, his ability to convert his experience into art, and exemplifies this skill in an intricate part-song for a chorus of men of good will. Far from being a rambling series of loosely connected episodes, it demonstrates how "Man reaches, stumbles forward, painfully, mistakenly sometimes." The novel is a tribute to the men like Doc who stumble forward and not, as is sometimes assumed, to Mack and the boys, who, as Mack himself tells Doc, "won't remember nothin' . . . won't learn nothin'."

Steinbeck's thesis about most of the inhabitants of Cannery Row is that their condition is superior to that of the ordinary respectable person, but even their condition leaves much to be desired. The admirable character is Doc; and it is entirely clear from the essay "About Ed Ricketts," in case anyone had any lingering doubts, that Doc in *Cannery Row* is a picture of Ricketts, to whom Steinbeck dedicated the book. The influence of Ricketts on Steinbeck's whole life and work is incalculable, but certainly *Cannery Row* makes it clear that Steinbeck regarded Ricketts as the most nearly ideal figure he had met—the heroic symbol of human potentialities wisely utilized. It is not necessary to summarize what Steinbeck found admirable about Ricketts; he has spoken for himself in novel and essay. All that needs to be observed in finally describing the "design" of *Cannery Row* is that at the time of his extreme disheartenment by what he had seen of war, Steinbeck sought his own escape into sanity by devising an allegory that would share with others his concept of the highest human potentiality.

CHAPTER *12*

The Defective Pearl

STEINBECK seemingly exhausted his passions by pouring his sharpest complaints and most cherished convictions into the intricate mould for *Cannery Row,* for he has never since recaptured the spirit that makes the novel glow like a homing beacon in a drab world. It should have been regarded as an ominous sign that his next work of fiction, *The Pearl,* was deemed suitable fare in 1945 for a woman's magazine—a bulwark of the very respectability pilloried in *Cannery Row*— and was published in a "tie-in" edition in 1947 at the time of the release of a motion picture adapted from it.

Brendan Gill in his review of Faulkner's *A Fable* in the *New Yorker* cynically supposes a conversation around a Hollywood swimming-pool that might have provided the inspiration for that ponderous book; it is not difficult to imagine *The Pearl* developing from similar chatter in a luxurious East Side New York apartment about writing something to tap the rich resources of the never-to-be-underestimated magazines for the homemaker.

Certainly in manufacturing *The Pearl* Steinbeck seems not to have had his mind on what he wished to say (as in *Cannery Row*), but his eye on what the market would bear. If he tried to appeal to a general audience, he succeeded; for the easily read *Pearl* has been one of his most popular books. From the viewpoint of admirers of *The Grapes of Wrath* and *Cannery Row,* however, it is not just a disappointment but a betrayal.

Like Hemingway's *Old Man and the Sea, The Pearl* is a twice-told tale, based on a legend Steinbeck picked up during his biological expedition to the Gulf of California and reported in *The Sea of Cortez*. In the original version, an Indian fisher-boy supposes that he will be able to sell a great pearl he finds for enough to let him loaf the rest of his life. When he tries to sell the pearl, however, the buyers try to cheat him. When he refuses to sell, he is beaten and tortured. Cursing the pearl, he throws it back into the sea and becomes once more a free man.

Steinbeck considered the legend "too reasonable to be true," although he said that he thought it probably was. In appropriating the tale for a commercial market, he tampered with it in a manner that did make it incredible. Hemingway had, of course, in transforming his great fish story made his hero stoical and indomitable instead of hysterically confused; but Steinbeck made even more wholesale changes in his source with more disastrous results.

In *The Pearl* the young diver is a discontented married man, eager for social advancement, who, when the town's decadent doctor refuses to treat his baby for a scorpion bite, strikes the doctor's gate "a crushing blow with his fist." Still rankled, he goes about his business and finds in a great oyster "the greatest pearl in the world." Like the fisher-boy in the original legend, he finds that the pearl buyers try to cheat him, he is plagued and tortured by would-be robbers and assassins, and he ultimately hurls the pearl back into the sea.

His motivation, however, is different. The anonymous boy in the legend sees the gem as providing the ability "to be drunk as long as he wished, to marry any one of a number of girls . . . [and to] purchase masses sufficient to pop him out of Purgatory like a squeezed watermelon seed." On the other hand Kino of the novel sees his catch providing the opportunity for him and his wife to be married "in the church," to buy new clothes, and to send his son to school—objectives that would no doubt be more acceptable than the anonymous fisherman's to the readers of the *Woman's Home Companion*. Talk of throwing the pearl back into the sea originates with Juana, Kino's wife, as soon as it becomes apparent that there are those who will stop at nothing to separate the diver from the pearl. Kino will have none of such talk, however, because, in his own somewhat baroque language, "the pearl has become my soul."

Kino's brother worries, however, because Kino has "defied not the pearl buyers, but the whole structure, the way of life." In *Cannery Row,* such defiance was an occasion for rejoicing, but Steinbeck has lost his inclination to rock the boat. Kino is unmoved by beatings, the destruction of his boat, and the burning of his house; but he is persuaded to dispose of the pearl and accept the *status quo* when his baby son is accidentally killed by his tormentors. He returns to town, not stealthily like the boy in the legend, but heralded by small hysterical boys left over from a victory parade. He offers Juana the chance to throw the pearl in the sea; but when she indicates that this is man's work, he flings it himself into the "lovely green water." This gesture has been widely admired as symbolizing a rejection of materialism. Unfortunately, that is not all it symbolizes. The reader is led to believe that Kino has not only rejected materialism but accepted the whole way of life he hoped to escape. The gesture may be interpreted not only as noble renunciation, but also as defeatism. Kino is akin not to Doc, but to the groundhog of *Cannery Row.*

One objection to this melodramatic film scenario, complete with recipes for the background music, is that to justify—barely—its separate publication, the book was made far longer than the material warranted. Compared to *Cannery Row*—a novel with a Dickensian, almost Joycean texture—*The Pearl* is turgid, overinflated. The fable would have provided about enough material—though hardly the right kind—for an interchapter in *Cannery Row.* Steinbeck's readers, like T. S. Eliot's, were beginning to get short weight.

A more serious objection is the reversal and refutation in this book of viewpoints that Steinbeck had advanced in more substantial works. *The Pearl* refutes, in the first place, the assumption underlying *Tortilla Flat* that there is no turning back the clock. Kino and Danny are somewhat similar; but Steinbeck's point about Danny is that, once he knows the responsibilities of property, he cannot return to a state of primitive innocence. Both novels involve the question that T. S. Eliot asks in "Gerontion": "After such knowledge, what forgiveness?" In *Tortilla Flat,* Steinbeck had replied, with Thomas Wolfe and other scions of the lost generation, "You can't go home again"; but in *The Pearl,* he says one can.

The book is a refutation, too, of the passionate credo that lies at the heart of *The Grapes of Wrath*:

> . . . man reaches, stumbles forward, painfully, mistakenly sometimes. Having stepped forward, he may slip back, but only half a step, never the full step back. . . . Fear the time when the bombs stop falling while the bombers live—for every bomb is proof that the spirit has not died . . . fear the time when Manself will not suffer and die for a concept, for this one quality is the foundation of Manself. . . .

In *The Pearl,* the bombs do stop falling while the bombers live. The time has come when Manself will not suffer and die for a concept. Kino suffers, but does not die; and surely if his is "the pearl of the world," he is "'Manself." Having stepped forward painfully, he slips back not just half a step, but toboggans to the very bottom of the heap, for his boat smashed, his baby dead, and the pearl cast into the sea, he has less when the story is over than he had when it started. It is true that he has learned to reject the shoddy material benefits he sought, but there is no indication that he has learned that there might be other alternatives than accepting these or sinking all the way back into his old way of life. Neither he nor the author recognizes the faulty dilemma. *The Pearl* would not contradict *The Grapes of Wrath* if Kino's pretensions to respectability were treated satirically, but they are not. The reader is apparently expected to sympathize with him as a man misused by a cold, hard world; the same effect could be achieved by having Connie Rivers rather than Tom Joad the hero of *The Grapes of Wrath*.

Contrasts might be drawn between *The Pearl* and other Steinbeck novels, but the abrupt change of tone it represents is best illustrated by comparing it with *Cannery Row*. Peter Lisca says that in the earlier book "Mack and the boys have thrown the jewel of great price back into the sea" before the story begins; but there is really no evidence that they ever found a pearl. Their withdrawal from competitive society is a gesture of resignation, not of rejection. Had they found a pearl, their characters suggest that they—like the finder in the original legend—would have regarded it as an opportunity to buy a life (and afterlife, if they believed in one) of ease for themselves; and they probably would have, like him, given it up undramatically if it appeared that it would be more trouble than it was worth. Kino is cut from a different cloth. He is not clever but lazy like Mack of the Palace Flophouse; he is much more like Mac, the labor organizer in *In Dubious Battle*, self-dramatizing and short-tempered. Actually a hot-headed primitive thrust into a mature world with which he is not prepared to cope, he most nearly resembles Pepe of "Flight."

Of course a writer has the right to change his mind; what Steinbeck says in *The Pearl*, like what he says in *Cannery Row*, is his business. One's right to say what one pleases, though, does not make all one's ideas equally acceptable to others or artistically fruitful. The reader who admires the dynamic, unfettered thinking of the principal figures in *The Grapes of Wrath* and *Cannery Row* is repulsed by the defeatism of *The Pearl*—just as some readers, disturbed by the praise of restlessness and enlightenment in the earlier novels, may admire the characters who learn to accept their place in *The Pearl*.

One can, however, cite something more concrete than mere opinion to support his description of *The Pearl* as artistically inferior to most of Steinbeck's previous works. In the first place, it is a melodrama. The distinguishing characteristic that makes melodrama generally an inferior art form is an illogically happy ending. The original fable Steinbeck reported was not melodrama, but low comedy. Its point was that the finder of the pearl hoped it would make life easier and more secure for him; when he learned the jewel was more trouble than it was worth, he got rid of it. The fable is consistent—probably why Steinbeck supposed it "too reasonable"—because what the principal character wants throughout is the greatest reward for the least effort. It is a comedy because the pearl to him is never more than a means to an end; and, the means proving a bother, the end is abandoned. How Steinbeck shifted this originally comic fable into one that should end tragically to be consistent is best shown by continuing the comparison of his version with his earlier short story "Flight."

Both Pepe and Kino are headstrong and able but ignorant young men. Both are prematurely called upon to cope with problems their training has not prepared them to solve. Both

are insulted—Pepé by taunts; Kino, by the offers of the pearl
buyers. Both react to the insults hastily without considering
whether they are prepared to accept the consequences of their
action. Neither is. Both make an ill-planned flight and are
pursued. Pepé is destroyed. In a Hollywood finish, however,
Kino eliminates his three pursuers and, though he loses his
child, returns to his village to make the grand gesture of throwing away the pearl. "Flight" is a meaningful naturalistic tragedy because, although the reader may sympathize with Pepé,
he should realize that the boy's position is logically hopeless.
Logic triumphs, but in *The Pearl* wishful thinking triumphs.

The problem is not really solved; Steinbeck leaves the impression at the end of *The Pearl* that all is forgiven and will be
forgotten. But is it? In a satisfactory comedy, loose ends are
tied up. There are too many left here. Kino has killed several
agents of his pursuers. Can he expect to go unpunished? Even
more important, can he really suppress his ambitions and
accept his former humble place? Steinbeck simply throws
these questions into the "lovely green water" along with the
pearl; the gesture of rejection at the end satisfies the reader
who feels that, after all, the simple life is best. This is soap
opera; as Maxwell Geismar aptly says, Steinbeck tends to
assign his primitives "a peculiar sort of suburban American
romanticism."

The reader who ponders over what he has read, however,
finds himself left with some perplexing questions; and not
questions like those posed by the end of *The Grapes of Wrath*,
which have no answers yet and which are outside the province
of the artist, but simply questions relevant to the allegory
that are left unanswered. *The Pearl*, not *The Grapes of Wrath*,
is the work of Steinbeck's which is left incomplete and whose
ending Edwin Burgum might justly call "fake symbolism"
prompted by "a meretricious desire to italicize the action."

It is impossible to account fully for the decline in Steinbeck's work that begins with *The Pearl*. Perhaps the war had
so disheartened him that he could no longer face the truth
about man's inhumanity; perhaps he was so eager to denounce
materialism that he failed to notice that in overstressing one
point he had confused others. Whatever the trouble, *The
Pearl* proved to be paste.

CHAPTER 13

The Lean Years

ALTHOUGH in some ways a meretricious work, *The Pearl,* because of its simplicity and anti-materialism, found admirers. Not even this much can be said for Steinbeck's next four novels—*The Wayward Bus, Burning Bright, East of Eden,* and *Sweet Thursday*—which have been, in different ways, failures. The shortcomings of these works have already been pointed out—some by their first reviewers; others by Peter Lisca, W. M. Frohock, and Charles C. Walcutt. If I could find what I considered adequate reasons to reverse the judgments of these earlier critics, I should be happy to present them; unfortunately, I have not. I can only regretfully concur in the judgment of my predecessors that Steinbeck's first four postwar novels are almost as embarrassingly bad as Wordsworth's late poems. Since there is little pleasure or even point in beating dead horses, I shall not treat these novels in as much detail as I have the earlier works, but shall point out only the deficiencies which I feel contribute to answering the overwhelming question, "What happened to John Steinbeck?"

I *A Wayward Pilgrimage*

Steinbeck wrote excitedly to his agents about his first major post-war novel, *The Wayward Bus,* but it is generally regarded as a distinct lapse on its author's part. What went wrong?

It is obvious from the moment one reads the prefatory quotation from *Everyman* and learns on the first page that the novel concerns a journey from Rebel Corners to San Juan de la Cruz that the book is an allegory. But almost all of his books had been allegories: some good, some bad. Why is this one best described as indifferent?

A successful allegorical novel functions on two levels, but these levels are fused because the allegory is inherent in the narrative rather than imposed upon it. Such a book is like a building in which the form is so perfectly suited to the function that nothing functionally necessary is sacrificed to demands of the design nor is the integrity of the design compromised to provide functional necessities. *The Red Pony* is an example of such a perfect fusion; but this fusion is not achieved in *The Wayward Bus*. Unless one is conscious that the work is allegorical, it seems intolerably meandering and pointless; yet if one reads it primarily as an allegory, the descriptions of the characters and scenery are overlong and often irrelevant.

Antonia Seixas explains the book as an outgrowth of Steinbeck's interest in non-teleological thinking[1]—the kind, discussed in the preface, concerned "not with what could be, or should be, or might be, but rather with what actually is." The author of a work that deals simply with the occurrence rather than the purpose of events strives to be entirely objective, as Steinbeck had been in *The Red Pony*, which deals with a boy's abandoning his illusions about what could or should be and recognizing what is. *The Wayward Bus* lacks objectivity, however, because Steinbeck's distaste for what he observed of post-war American society continually overwhelms his sense of detachment. While he shows us what he thinks *is,* he cannot keep from registering almost as much disgust with things he sees as Sinclair Lewis had. Since the scientist and satirist in Steinbeck constantly war with each other in the novel, *The Wayward Bus* is neither science, satire, nor a happy mixture of the two, but a shapeless tale neither moral, immoral, nor amoral enough to satisfy good, bad, or indifferent readers.

The key to Steinbeck's concept of post-war America is found in the palimpsest on the bumper of the wayward bus, which is described in the second chapter:

The front bumper of the bus had once borne the inscription, still barely readable, "el gran Poder de Jesus," "the great power of Jesus." But that had been painted on by a former owner. Now the simple word "Sweetheart" was boldly lettered on front and rear bumpers.

The two legends are slogans of particular eras. At one time the force guiding the world (and the owner of the bus) had been "the great power of Jesus," but this has been effaced. Society now cherishes the ideas symbolized by the colloquial "Sweetheart."

Out of context this palimpsest is easily misinterpreted. It might seem that Steinbeck is decrying the decline of Christianity, but his remarks in this novel and elsewhere about traditional religion make him an unlikely defender of the faith. What he implies is not that Christianity had been the *right* guide, but that it had been *a* guide. Ernest Horton, the Congressional Medal of Honor winner who now sells vulgar novelties, speaks for his creator when he says: "It don't make a bit of difference who you work for if you believe in it. . . . The government or anybody else." He echoes ideas expressed a century earlier in Matthew Arnold's "Pis-Aller."

Besides the inscription on the bus, there are many other decaying religious signs mentioned in the novel; the most prominent among them is a faded "REPENT" that had been painted with great effort on the side of a cliff below which the bus stops. It is implied that the efficacy of Christianity has been dissipated because it made claims that experience did not verify. As Horton explains, "honesty and thrift"— two virtues associated with traditional Christianity, especially in Puritan America—"didn't work out" and nothing has replaced them.

Actually, however, something has—something Steinbeck views with alarm. What has supplanted Christianity is a craving for material sweetness. One might first read the term "Sweetheart" painted on the bus as loaded with sexual implications and associate it with the lustful drives of several characters in the novel. It has, however, several other meanings, two of which are stressed in the novel. It summarizes the desires and prejudices of a group of characters who can face reality only when it is sugar-coated; and, as the motto of the bus driver, it symbolizes a detached Saroyanesque love of everything and everybody.

As far as the first of these meanings is concerned, it is noticeable that the only food the travelers have on their journey is four sickeningly sweet kinds of pie—raspberry, lemon cream, raisin, and caramel custard. Repeatedly, too, Steinbeck points out a single source for what ideas his characters boast. A strip-teaser who calls herself Camille Oaks, for example, envisions herself married: "She'd have a husband, of course, but she couldn't see him in her picture, because the advertising in the women's magazines from which her dreams came never included a man." "Pimples," Steinbeck writes of the bus driver's adolescent assistant, "took most of his ideas from moving pictures and the rest from the radio." The girls who work in a restaurant the bus driver operates "dreamed over movie magazines . . . sighed into the juke box." A capitalist's wife dreams of an orchid house she had seen in "an article in *Harper's Bazaar.*" The Bible has been replaced as a guide to life for the barely literate by the mass media and the gooey sweet picture of life they confect. Steinbeck pictures, like Philip Wylie in *Generation of Vipers,* a world about to smother in its own syrup.

If Steinbeck had been content to paint a satirical picture of the kind of vulgar society Ezra Pound had summed up in the third section of "Hugh Selwyn Mauberley" ("The Pianola 'replaces' Sappho's barbitos."), he might have denounced what *is* as vigorously as Wylie or Sinclair Lewis. He was not content, however, to satirize, as he had in *The Pastures of Heaven* and *Tortilla Flat,* the smug superficiality of the middle class. His troubles began when he forgot his non-teleology and sat down to write a prescription.

The world may still be if not saved, at least preserved, if those in the driver's seat accept it as it is and keep on going despite the difficulty of dealing with nasty and discourteous passengers. Juan Chicoy, the driver of the wayward bus, is tempted at one point to abandon his job to run off to Mexico. But when he does flee his responsibilities, he feels "miserable." After sexual intercourse with a capitalist's idealistic daughter, he goes back to the job.

The trouble lies in the characterization of Juan. As Peter Lisca points out, his initials, like Jim Casy's in *The Grapes of*

Wrath are the same as Jesus Christ's. Charles Walcutt explains in *American Literary Naturalism,* however, why Juan fails to live up to his symbolic billing:

> Juan's personal superiority is not justified. . . . He is . . . set up before us as a noble savage who can repair a bus and haul it out of a hole better than a typical American can do. There is something phoney in this sort of primitivism, for neither Juan's Mexican-Catholic roots nor his mechanical competence go deep enough to account for his superiority to the group of travelers.

Walcutt is right. Juan is one of Steinbeck's futile efforts to find an uneducated hero with the same qualities as Doc in *Cannery Row.* The trouble with this effort is that Doc's desirable qualities are the result of the discipline of his scientific training and his cultivated taste in the arts. Steinbeck has no more success than the eighteenth-century pursuers of the "noble savage" in proving that these qualities can be found in the untutored mind. Jim Casy, of course, displayed some, but only after he had rigorously disciplined himself. Steinbeck has no more success than Madison Avenue in proving that good nature is a substitute for training and self-discipline. Steinbeck's own natives in *The Pearl* and *The Forgotten Village* are enough evidence that a Mexican-Catholic background cannot itself provide such discipline. As for the merits of mechanical competence, Steinbeck himself had written scoffingly of "tinkerers." In *The Pastures of Heaven,* he satirized a boy to whom *science* meant "radios, archeology, and airplanes." Yet that is all *science* would mean if we are to believe that the scientific attitude is developed by tuning motors.

Juan's "tinkering" with one of his passengers is especially unconvincing. The "climax" of the story occurs when Juan finally copulates with Mildred Pritchard, with whom he has been flirting all through the novel. He is almost dispassionate about sex, although he does admit to Mildred that he left the bus in hopes that she might follow him. Is he, however, saying this just to be kind, as at the beginning of the novel he begins to call Pimples—named for his abundant skin blemishes— "Kit" to boost his ego? If he isn't, just what has become of his dispassion—he seems to have a very personal stake in interrupting the journey; but if he is dispassionate, why have there been so many earlier references to a sexual attraction between the pair? If Juan were really obliging Mildred just to demonstrate his universal love, his behavior would be more convincing if he had earlier been repelled by or at least indifferent to her.

His inexplicable behavior calls attention to another problem. If Juan has sexual relations with Mildred only for the sake of her morale—if he could really, as he says, "go without it for a while"—why are other forms of lack of discipline (like Pimples' pie-eating) not subject to scrutiny? And if Juan's motives are not so altruistic, just what is the book about but a concupiscent bus driver who takes time out to have a brief affair with a passenger? The trouble is not with the morality of the book, but with its artistry; if Juan really fornicates only for charitable purposes, few readers will be able to identify themselves emotionally with him. If, on the other hand, he doesn't, it is hard to see what allegorical significance the novel is supposed to have. As the book ends, it is neither fish nor fowl. One suspects that Steinbeck was thinking of sales and not dramatic necessity when he wound things up with a little roll in the hay.

II A Tiger by the Tail

Steinbeck solved the problem that had defeated him in *The Wayward Bus* of fusing a convincingly realistic narrative with a carefully articulated allegory by scuttling realism in his next work. The result was a pure allegory that is artistically negligible, but important to an understanding of the author's ideas.

Steinbeck was apparently genuinely hurt by the hostile reception of his play-novelette, *Burning Bright*. He still had enough faith in it after the criticisms appeared to defend its theme, form, and language in "Critics, Critics, Burning Bright,"[2] the most blistering answer he made to his critics. On sober second thought, however, he modified his views and admitted to Peter Lisca in 1954 that the work "was too abstract, that it preached too much, and that the audience was always a step ahead of it." It would be difficult to improve upon his criticism; for, even if Steinbeck's allegory had gone wrong, he remained capable of learning from his mistakes and, after recovering from his disappointment, of functioning as his own soundest critic.

Despite the obvious weaknesses of the work—the confusing structure and the artificial language—which make critics tend to pass over it quickly, it is important to an understanding of all Steinbeck's writing. It has often been observed that this work shows that Steinbeck, whose attitude towards society had frequently been negative, was capable of an affirmation, even if he could not find an artistically satisfying form in which to present it. It should also be observed that the characters in the book help to clarify the meaning of those in some of Steinbeck's other works.

The central character, Joe Saul, who finally rises to the affirmation of the brotherhood of the whole human family that ends the play—"Every man is father of all children"—is praised during the play for two reasons. First—although sterile and, until near the end of the play, proud and self-important—he is capable of great gentleness and affection; and secondly, he is master of a traditional craft with a deep but not boisterous respect for his calling and its long tradition. His attitude is apparent from the fault he finds—when he is depicted as a circus performer—with his young assistant: "You have not the infinite respect for your tools and your profession—Profession! You have made it a trade."

Looking back from the vantage point of this work in which Steinbeck labored for clarity, we can see that affection, skill, and respect have been the trait of all the really heroic men in his novels—Doctor Burton in *In Dubious Battle,* Slim in *Of Mice and Men,* Tom Joad in *The Grapes of Wrath,* Mayor Orden in *The Moon is Down,* Doc in *Cannery Row,* and Juan Chicoy in *The Wayward Bus.* Though *Burning Bright* differs in form from these works, it summarizes the view they have expressed of what it means to be a successful human being. Despite superficial diversity, there runs through Steinbeck's works a consistent philosophy of life.

The character of Victor, the assistant whom Joe Saul criticizes and the man who actually impregnates the wife, is also more important as a symbol of a consistent attitude in Steinbeck's work than has been generally observed. Steinbeck writes that it was "Victor's unfortunate choice . . . always to mis-see, to mis-hear, to misjudge." "His malformed wisdom," Steinbeck describes as "poolhall, locker-room, joke-book wisdom." The thing he lacks, as Joe Saul's wife tells him, is "affection"; and, since this lack keeps him out of a world other than that of physical sensation, he must "disbelieve" in the existence of any other.

Through Victor, Steinbeck makes explicit the weakness of the "villainous" characters in his other novels. In his statement that Victor "mis-sees, mis-hears, and misjudges" he states exactly what he shows in episode after episode in *The Pastures of Heaven* is the "curse" that hangs over the Munroes. These terms describe also the principal characteristics of Curley and his ill-fated wife in *Of Mice and Men,* of both the arrogant fruit-growers and the overly impetuous labor organizers in *In Dubious Battle,* Jody's well-intentioned but limited father in *The Red Pony,* the fanatical invaders in *The Moon is Down,* the respectable citizens concerned about Josh Billings' insides in *Cannery Row,* and the greedy buyers in *The Pearl.* As is shown in the Lopez sisters' episode and other incidents in *The Pastures of Heaven,* Bert Munroe's wisdom is also a "poolhall, joke-book" wisdom. Finally the statement about Victor's being locked out of a world recalls the angry passage in *The Grapes of Wrath* in which Steinbeck speaks of "the quality of owning" that freezes the owners "forever into I" and cuts them off from the "we"—universal brotherhood.

One thing that has changed during the course of Steinbeck's literary career is his opinion about the probable survival of these perceptually deficient people. In his most cynical periods during the depression, it appeared to him that these people without affection might triumph. Later he became skeptical of their chances; and, finally in this affirmative novel, he indicated that he thought not only that they would be destroyed but that they must be if "virtue" were to triumph.

Peter Lisca, speaking for other critics, has complained about Victor's being "denied the fellowship of man that the book preaches" when he is drowned near the end of the novel by Joe Saul's friend. Lisca calls his being put unconscious on an outbound ship in the slightly revised play-version "a make-shift improvement." From the viewpoint of artistic consistency, it is not an improvement at all, but a concession that weakens the allegory. Steinbeck originally had taken a strictly non-teleological view of the matter and shown that, from the viewpoint of biological evolution, there were organisms that might make a contribution to the continuation of the species (Victor came from strong stock) but that were incapable of learning to adjust themselves to changed conditions. Victor's final demand that the wife flee with him shows his intellectual incapacity and indicates that, since he cannot learn, he must—from the viewpoint of "natural selection"—be destroyed as a predator.

The treatment of Victor suggests a clear-cut distinction between Steinbeck's conception of which characteristics may be hereditary and which environmentally acquired: the strength, the agility of the father are physical characteristics that Victor's son may acquire, but placing him in an environment of affection and respect may engraft him on to a great human tradition and make him not just the son of one "mis-seeing" man, but of every perceptive man. Steinbeck's point then appears to be that Friend Ed destroys Victor not for personal but social reasons; and the author would probably say of Ed, as of Doc in *Cannery Row,* "he can kill anything for need but he could not even hurt a feeling for pleasure." The idea is not inconsistent with Steinbeck's theories about universal brotherhood, but whether it is acceptable to the individual reader is another matter.

The other two members of the small cast of this drama also recall characters in Steinbeck's other works. Friend Ed's similarity to Doc in *Cannery Row* has just been pointed out. His solving of the problem that threatens to break up the family and his then shaming Joe Saul into behaving nobly also recalls Casy, who preserved the Joad family by allowing Tom to escape after the fight at the Hooverville and introduced him to the idea of working for humanity. The wife Mordeen, who is not especially "virtuous" in the conventional sense of the word, but who is willing to make any sacrifice out of her great love for her husband, finds her prototype in Ma Joad, of whom Casy said: "There's a woman so great with love—she scares me."

These similarities to the much more complex *Grapes of Wrath* serve to point out the basic similarity between the themes of the two works, both of which argue that man's fundamental responsibility is not to his own "fambly" or "blood" but to all of humanity. People had missed the point in the longer novel; but, when in *Burning Bright,* they could not miss it, they justifiably rejected the oversimplified vehicle.

III *Patchwork Leviathan*

Discouraged by the thinness of Steinbeck's short works in the late forties, readers had been looking forward with interest to a long-promised "major" work. While they were not entirely dissatisfied with what they found when *East of Eden* appeared in 1952, they were hardly convinced of its merits. Like *Burning Bright*, the new novel conveyed an affirmatively and undeniably noble message about the necessity of never giving up the struggle to survive; but did the end justify the means—the length, the disorganization, and the sensationalism of the book? The answer seems to be *no.* Certainly the vast hulk lacks the immediate impact and metaphorical unity of *The Grapes of Wrath.* As in his two preceding works, Steinbeck seems to have been unable to fuse form and content.

Much the same thing seems to have happened to Steinbeck while he was working on this novel that Howard Vincent in *The Trying-Out of Moby Dick* theorizes happened to Melville when—possibly under Hawthorne's influence—he decided to turn a simple narrative of a whaling voyage into his great allegory symbolizing man's struggle with the incomprehensible forces of nature.

According to Laura Hobson, writing in the *Saturday Review* at the time *East of Eden* appeared, Steinbeck began the novel about the time he finished *The Wayward Bus* as a record for his two small sons of their ancestors' movement westward after the Civil War into the Salinas Valley. The story—which would have dealt with Steinbeck's mother's family, the Hamiltons—was to have been told in the first person. Traces of the original material may be observed in those passages of the novel in which a first-person narrator speaks to his children; and Steinbeck's mother, other relatives, and even Steinbeck himself as a child appear briefly. As Peter Lisca observes, however, "Somewhere in the early stages of this family saga . . . Steinbeck introduced a fictional family, the Trasks, and he soon found himself at the mercy of his materials." Whatever the reason for the change of his plans, it was not for the better. The fragments of the original Hamilton story are far better reading than the unlikely Trask legend.

While I would hesitate to predict that the same belated fame that awaited *Moby Dick* awaits *East of Eden*, there is another important similarity between the novels—both concern the self-destruction of a monomaniac. Both Captain Ahab and Cathy Trask, the wayward wife and successful brothel-keeper in *East of Eden*, are single-mindedly bent on exercising their wills, are ready to destroy anything that stands in their way, and will scruple nothing to achieve their ends. Both are also clever enough to manipulate other people in order to achieve their purposes, and both are responsible for their own destruction. Here the similarity ends; for the focusing upon a monomaniac that crystallized Melville's vision seems to have dissipated Steinbeck's.

The famous "strike through the mask speech" illuminates Ahab's motives; but in *East of Eden* Cathy's are never clarified. The only time she really speaks for herself is in a conversation with her husband, who has just discovered after eleven years' separation that she is still in the neighborhood. When he asks her if she means that "in the whole world there's only evil and folly?" she replies: "That's exactly what I mean." After showing him pictures that illustrate the depraved tastes of the community's leading citizens, she continues: "Do you think I want to be human? Look at those pictures! I'd rather be a dog than a human. But I'm not a dog. I'm smarter than humans. Nobody can hurt me." She has sacrificed all human affections to her desire for power and revenge. It is not clear, however, what has driven her to this position. In the interview with her husband, she attributes her behavior to her treatment by the owner of a chain of brothels who had beaten her nearly to death. The narrator has earlier informed us, however, that she behaved just as "inhumanly" before she had met this man.

Steinbeck further confuses the picture of Cathy by editorializing about her in two places early in the book. He introduces her—probably inaccurately—as a girl who would formerly have been spoken of as "possessed by a devil" and expresses the opinion that she is a "psychic monster . . . born with the tendencies, or lack of them, which drove and forced her all of her life." Later, however, he wonders if his own observation is true, admitting that "since we cannot know what she wanted, we will never know whether or not she got it. . . . Her life may have been her language, formal, developed, indecipherable. It is easy to say she was bad, but there is little meaning unless we know why."

As a non-teleological thinker, Steinbeck is on sound ground in both passages; but good science is not necessarily good fiction. What Steinbeck seemingly does not realize is that, whether we understand the reasons for certain patterns of behavior or not, they are going to have consequences about which we must do something. We can see where such behavior leads and avoid it if we do not wish to go there. *East of Eden* suffers, however, from the author's inability to make up his mind whether he is pleading (as his first passage about Cathy suggests) for suspension of judgment in the absence of reliable knowledge or (as his second passage suggests) throwing up his hands and saying the situation is hopeless. Either might provide an impressive basis for a novel, but the two do not mix.

The treatment of the motivation of anti-social behavior is further confused by Steinbeck's discussion of another "criminal type," Cathy's assistant Joe, who had "built his hatreds little by little—beginning with a mother who neglected him, a father who alternately whipped and slobbered over him" into a "lonely set of rules" for getting revenge on a world he hated. In his picture of Joe, Steinbeck seems to be following a conventional line of many sociologically oriented writers who believe that "bad boys and girls are made, not born."

What is difficult to fathom is why the same principle could not have applied to Cathy, especially since Joe is responsible for her defeat and since, thinking over her past when she realizes that the Joes of the world are after her, Cathy recalls that as a child "smarter and prettier than anyone else," she sometimes had "a lonely fear . . . that she seemed surrounded by a tree-tall forest of enemies."

The trouble with the inconsistent treatment of Cathy and Joe is not that anti-social behavior can be indisputably explained but that, if *East of Eden* were to have any unity, Steinbeck should either have fixed upon one interpretation of her behavior and stuck to it or not have attempted any and simply explained non-teleologically what she *did* and how it affected other people. It is difficult to explain Steinbeck's presenting himself as knowing Joe's motivation and not Cathy's unless we assume that he is confusing real life and fiction. Since an author, after all, chooses his own characters, the reader expects him to have some consistent concept of his relationship to them. What seems to have happened is that Steinbeck's inability to reconcile his propensity for detached scientific observation with his growing tendency to pontificate kept him from perceiving the inconsistencies in *East of Eden.*

Cathy's death is as inexplicable as her life. When Captain Ahab is caught in his own toils, he goes down fighting and drags with him almost a whole shipful of allegorical representatives of a variety of naive philosophies. Cathy, on the other hand, commits suicide when she supposes that, even if she can outwit Joe, she will eventually be outwitted by someone else of her own ilk. Furthermore, she carries no one to destruction with her. The damning photographs she has been accumulating which would destroy many men fall fortuitously into the hands of a wise and kindly sheriff who destroys them. Her death is not, like Ahab's, a catastrophe, but an unmixed blessing to the community.

The suicide is, furthermore, entirely inconsistent with Cathy's character as developed in the rest of the book. The youthful fears that supposedly motivate it are not mentioned elsewhere—certainly not in the portrayal of her shrewish childhood—so that the reader is unprepared for and unconvinced by them. The salvation of those who might have been destroyed with her is entirely gratuitous. The result is not tragedy or comedy, but—as in *The Pearl*—melodrama.

Steinbeck may have been trying, of course, to put across the idea that paranoia will destroy itself without disrupting society. But even if we were not convinced of the unsoundness of this notion by the fictitious Ahab, the historical Hitler and others would make Steinbeck's sugar-coated moral difficult to swallow. One wonders, for example, what might happen if a person of Cathy's disposition had nuclear weapons at her disposal. One sees in *East of Eden* what may be wrong with *The Moon is Down;* Steinbeck could not face unblinkingly the possible consequences of an unchecked lust for power. He seems to have written with his eye on the lending library rather than the concentration camp.

Cathy Trask is not the only important figure in *East of Eden,* but I have dealt with her confusing and finally sentimental history at length because she is the most conspicuous and provocative figure in the novel. It is fair to judge the novel on the basis of the Cathy story, because, while a novel might be great despite disgressions and irrelevancies, I do not believe that it can be judged artistically successful if a principal character is treated so contradictorily that she lacks significance. I fail to find, furthermore, that the other important characters are any more consistently realized than Cathy.

As for the long discussions of the meaning of the Cain and Abel story, centering around the interpretation of the Hebrew word "Timshel" (an obscure term occurring in the Lord's rejection of Cain's sacrifice),[3] I do not think Steinbeck succeeds in making all the talk dramatically convincing. The theological disputation is interesting as an exposition of Steinbeck's ideas, but these lack consistency and might be more appropriately discussed in an essay than a novel. Those interested in Steinbeck's unsuccessful battle with the question of free will should turn to the detailed critique of the structural and philosophical weaknesses of the novel in Peter Lisca's *The Wide World of John Steinbeck.*

IV *Sellout*

Steinbeck's prodigious labors to bring order to his intractable materials in *East of Eden* must have exhausted him. He must also have suspected that his efforts had been largely in vain since he did not try to defend this novel as he had

Burning Bright. Instead he sought release in a light-hearted farce unweighted with allegorical significance. Unfortunately, he chose for his setting to return to Cannery Row which he had exploited triumphantly when seeking refuge from the disillusions of war. *Sweet Thursday,* not much in itself, appears even poorer than it otherwise might when contrasted with its predecessor.

Since almost every critic has found *Sweet Thursday* a tired book, there is little reason to belabor its inferiority to *Cannery Row.* It need only be pointed out that Steinbeck here for the first time in his career repeated himself by using not only old sets and characters, but even the framework of the earlier novel—the gradual build-up to a much-anticipated but disastrous party followed by general depression and a break in events that starts the action toward a triumphant conclusion. He also repeats not once but twice the dramatically effective device he had used in "The Snake" to indicate the effect a woman is having upon a man by having his absorption in what she is saying or doing make him miss a necessary step in the preparation of a series of biological slides.

The major difference between the two novels is the treatment of Doc, a sore subject that Peter Lisca discusses at length in *The Wide World of John Steinbeck.* He does not show, however, how the denouement of *Sweet Thursday* completely contradicts the conclusion of *Cannery Row.* The point of the last two chapters of the earlier novel is that man is different from the other animals—specifically from the "well-grown gopher," the symbol of the purely physical being —since man has consciousness, which gives him the ability to recall and re-create experience, to triumph through a disciplined use of his artistic capacities over the loneliness and isolation of the purely sensual being.

This idea is simply discarded in *Sweet Thursday,* which is concerned with the effort of Doc to get the woman he "needs." Doc even says of the "hustler" (*Sweet Thursday* abounds in euphemisms) from the Bear Flag Restaurant who has captured his heart that if he fails to get her, he will "never be a whole man," but will live "a gray half-life and . . . mourn for my lost girl every hour of the rest of my life." The wilted "Black Marigolds" have been consigned to the trash-can.

Sweet Thursday is not just different, however, from *Cannery Row;* it is genuinely anti-intellectual if we define anti-intellectualism as the belief that problems are solved by force and violence rather than reason. The novel is anti-intellectual because the denouement—the union of Doc and his Suzy—is brought about not by intelligent action but by a subnormal character's breaking Doc's arm with a baseball bat. Since this violence produces the desired effect, the reader is probably supposed to sympathize with it; but it is hard to see how this behavior differs from that of the sniper in the window who shot Joy in *In Dubious Battle* or from that of the vigilantes who burned the Hooverville in *The Grapes of Wrath.*

The anti-intellectualism of *Sweet Thursday* is, furthermore, not that of contemporary pessimists like Faulkner who appear to doubt most men's capacity to reason. It is rather that of the fatuously melodramatic nineteenth-century road show, which was based on the assumption that if one is sweet, one doesn't have to be bright. Once Doc gets his girl, he also gets, through the intervention of a most unlikely *deus ex machina,* the promise of a nice appointment at the California Institute of Technology. The gopher chapter of *Cannery Row* was wrong; one can have both sex and security.

While *Sweet Thursday* has been found a tired book, it has not been noticed that it is also a cantankerous book—a work that does not satirize those who delude and hurt themselves, but rather complains peevishly about those who annoy the author personally. There are three evidences that Steinbeck, who in his finest works advocated selflessness, was becoming increasingly more concerned with his own crotchets than with the state of mankind.

The first of these is the handling of the inter-chapters in *Sweet Thursday.* There are only two, and neither is really related to the main story. Both "The Great Roque War" and "The Butterfly Festivals" are malicious attacks not on middle-class respectability in general, but on Pacific Grove, California, in particular. Since Steinbeck had lived in that pietistic town in comparative poverty for a number of years, one suspects he may have taken advantage of an opportunity to grind a personal axe. These suspicions are heightened by some of the speeches of an improbable character, old Jingleballicks, devised especially as *deus ex machina.*

At first the old man seems merely another of Steinbeck's burlesques of the greedy and grasping middle-class; but the satire loses its bite when this character paves Doc's road to security. What is particularly suspicious about Steinbeck's motives for introducing this character is a long speech on the income tax that he might have lifted directly from Little Orphan Annie's Daddy Warbucks:

> "The only creative thing we have is the individual, but the law doesn't permit me to give money to an individual. I must give it to a group, an organization—and the only thing a group has ever created is bookkeeping. To participate in my gift, the individual must become part of the group and thus lose his individuality and his creativeness. . . . Why, if you, through creative work, should win a prize, most of the money would go in taxes."

These remarks could be a satirical thrust at the great philanthropical bureaucracies of the post-war era, but they are too oversimplified to have much satirical impact. When one considers that Steinbeck is one of those who had won prizes "through creative work," the argument sounds suspiciously like special pleading. In fact, one wonders if Steinbeck, having profited from Hollywood and the book clubs, had not decided, while still detesting the middle-class, that it was all right so long as it was supporting him.

The most cantankerous parts of *Sweet Thursday,* however, concern a character who was dropped entirely when the novel was converted into the musical comedy *Pipe Dream.* Joe Elegant, cook at the Bear Flag Restaurant, is writing a novel in his spare time. Joe clearly satirizes not just a type of person, but a particular rival writer, as is apparent from the parallels between *Other Voices, Other Rooms* and the famous publicity photograph of Truman Capote and the following passage:

> The book was going well. His hero had been born in a state of shock and nothing subsequent reassured him. When a symbol wasn't slapping him in the mouth, a myth was kicking

his feet out from under him. It was a book of moods, of dank rooms with cryptic wallpaper, of pale odors, of decaying dreams. . . . Joe Elegant was beginning to plan his photograph for the back of the dust cover: open collar, he thought, and a small wry smile, and one hand relaxed in front of him with an open poison ring on the third finger.

Some of Steinbeck's remarks about Joe Elegant, however, unfortunately boomerang. Another character, for example, asks Joe, "Whyn't you a write a story about something real?" Surely the same question could have been asked Steinbeck after he had written *Burning Bright* or the Trask story in *East of Eden*. Joe also thinks that "he would go to Rome after his book was published." The reference to the flight of many young writers like Capote and Tennessee Williams to Italy after establishing themselves with lurid local color stories is obvious; yet, Steinbeck had not only made a number of trips to Europe himself, but had also deserted the region he knew and wrote about best for New York and Paris after achieving success.

Steinbeck evidently failed to perceive that some of his most ill-natured thrusts at the Joe Elegants of the contemporary literary scene applied to himself. His attitude, however, explains much about the whole tenor of *Sweet Thursday*. Having failed in his last several novels to produce satisfactory allegories, Steinbeck had apparently decided to abandon the lonely pursuit of artistic excellence and write something funny for the folks. It is difficult to believe, however, that he could really have believed in what he was doing; *Sweet Thursday* is an insensitive book by a disgruntled man, and it is hard to think that it was written out of anything but a vast contempt for reviewers and readers alike. The irony is that this attempt to exploit crude public tastes was not chosen by any book clubs and not purchased for hundreds of thousands of dollars by Hollywood. Even the musical comedy based upon it was not the hoped-for "sellout", but was classified by *Variety* as a "flop."

CHAPTER 14

Mr. Steinbeck Goes to Town

MAXWELL GEISMAR emphasizes in *American Moderns* that the real question about John Steinbeck is what has happened to him. Why has there been a steady decline in the quality of his work since the end of World War II? Why is this man, once acclaimed one of our two or three greatest writers and considered for the Nobel Prize, sometimes today not even regarded as a serious writer?

The decline is undeniable; some causes of it, obvious. Certainly the things that Peter Lisca mentions—the death of Ed Ricketts and Steinbeck's move from California to the big city—are important. Until more information becomes available, it will not be possible to determine the extent of Ricketts' influence; but certainly the marine biologist served as both tutor and critic. *Cannery Row* and "About Ed Ricketts" show the extent of Steinbeck's admiration, and it is apparent that no one has taken Ricketts' place. We may speculate that if Ricketts were still influencing Steinbeck, he might work more carefully and be less pontifical. Yet while Ricketts' death might explain a change in the tone of Steinbeck's writing and even the lack of adequate criticism of some recent manuscripts, it could not satisfactorily account for the increasing abstractness of Steinbeck's thought or the increasing insensitivity of his language.

Steinbeck unquestionably started downhill when he left California, for his best books deal with persons and places he knew intimately. After making several false starts, of which only *Cup of Gold* and *To a God Unknown* were published, he wrote his distinguished books—*The Pastures of Heaven, In Dubious Battle, Of Mice and Men, The Red Pony, The*

Grapes of Wrath—about the things that were physically and spiritually closest to him. In *The Moon is Down* he tried to widen the scope of his work, but his observations of the war discouraged him—he was not yet ready to face unblinkingly the world at large. He had seen, however, that there was a larger world; and since he was making money, he no longer wished to be confined to his valley. He was still operating on the momentum of his experiences during the thirties when he capped his career with *Cannery Row*, but it was a gone world he conjured up.

In his next several books—*The Pearl, The Wayward Bus, Burning Bright*—allegory overwhelmed experience and a flirtation with existentialism clashed with his satirical tendencies, so that by the time he came to write *East of Eden* he no longer trusted his memories and overloaded what might have been a moving pastoral with an elaborate and befuddled allegory. The best things in this big novel, the fragments of the Hamilton story, show, however, the effect of Steinbeck's long separation from the speech of his native region.

He is not a man, like Joyce Cary, for example, who can satisfactorily summon an emotionally charged remembrance of things past. Like other scientists, he must move his eye constantly back and forth between his specimen and his sketch pad. When his eye is too long off its subject, his reproductions lose fidelity, just as the recollections of his characters, beginning with Sir Henry Morgan, become exaggerated as time passes. It takes a long time, however, as Vladimir Nabokov demonstrates, to learn enough about a new place and a new people and their idiom to write about them as effectively as one wrote about his old subjects in his old tongue.

Sweet Thursday made it evident that Steinbeck had lost touch with his California experience, yet remained too much a satirist to produce successfully the kind of soothing syrups the mass media demanded. He is not a man who can live tranquilly with his memories; whatever he does, he will not write a *Doctor Zhivago*. Although he shares with Boris Pasternak a transcendental concept of man's capacities, even his preoccupation with non-teleological thinking has not given him the capacity for detachment that distinguishes the indomitable spirit of that modern Olympian.

Steinbeck's increasing loss of touch with his subject matter also spawned another trouble—one that always plagues the allegorist who, like an executive, may become too far removed from the operations in which he discerns and upon which he imposes a pattern to make it relevant to present problems. An anonymous *Time* reviewer of *Lifeboat,* the Alfred Hitchcock film for which Steinbeck wrote the script, summed up what might be said of much of Steinbeck's later work when he called the film:

> . . . a remarkably intelligent picture almost totally devoid of emotion. Its characters are not so much real people, derelicts upon a real sea, as they are a set of propositions in a theorem. This story is an adroit allegory of world shipwreck.

The problem of the allegorist is to maintain the proper balance between science and sensitivity, between the demands of the pattern and the demand of the audience for emotions it can share. Not all Steinbeck's later allegories were adroit. The curious thing is that Steinbeck has often been charged with sentimentality, an overabundance of false emotion, whereas the fault that has plagued much of his work since *Cannery Row* has been an insensitivity—or a preoccupation with manipulating patterns rather than presenting people— that led to the aridity of *Burning Bright* and the anti-intellectualism of *Sweet Thursday.* Only in *East of Eden* do we find him sacrificing what would be likely to what would be nice. What Steinbeck failed to realize in constructing his later allegories is that it is very unlikely that an author can interest the audience in the fate of characters in whom he himself does not appear interested as more than symbols. Part of the trouble in Steinbeck's post-war books is that he appears to have become detached from his characters because he has been avoiding reality. He has sometimes taken refuge, I suspect, in non-teleological thinking because he has lacked the sophistication to ask "why" people behaved in certain ways— the answer might be too disturbing. When Steinbeck was asked why he wrote, he replied that basically he did so because he liked to.[1] This is, of course, all the reason one needs; it is certainly this attitude that has given the world some of its most enjoyable art.

What Steinbeck may be unable to face, however, is the possibility that people like the growers in *The Grapes of Wrath* and the invaders in *The Moon is Down* and even Cathy in *East of Eden* also do what they do because they like to. It takes an absolutely first-rate literary intelligence like the too-little-honored H. H. Munro ("Saki") to theorize (as he did in "Filboid Studge") that "there are people who might *like* to kill their neighbors now and then." The point is not that Saki is *right* about this aspect of human behavior; but that, if we are going to be truly detached and objective in our thinking, we must entertain every hypothesis that might explain a phenomenon, no matter how repugnant.

Edmund Wilson was wrong, therefore, when he said in *The Boys in the Back Room* that Steinbeck was first-rate in his "unpanicky scrutiny of life." He had been when he wrote *In Dubious Battle* and *Of Mice and Men*, but not afterwards. What has been first-rate about Steinbeck is his ability—the rare one that we so much need and so seldom find in teachers —to find concrete metaphors through which to communicate successfully abstract ideas. Steinbeck found these metaphors in his remarkably perceptive, rather than his remarkably objective, scrutiny of his native California valleys. He has lacked, however, the sophistication to perceive as calmly the world into which success has carried him.

As Steinbeck has become further removed from the world he knew, he seems also—perhaps because his new surroundings intimidated him—to have grown increasingly touchy and disgruntled about the reception of his work. The critics— whose good will he almost certainly desires despite his condescending attitude towards them—and the public consistently missed the point of his early books. When he began to make money, he must have been understandably attracted by the security it offered. If readers didn't understand what he had to say anyway, why not settle for cash? When he wrote what he thought would pay instead of what he wished, he had, however, to "split" before civilization.

Perhaps no writer has predicted his own course as well as Steinbeck did in his first novel, *Cup of Gold*. There Merlin tells young Henry Morgan that he may become a great man as long as he remains a little boy. During the thirties, Steinbeck succeeded, as is shown by the simple types of people he wrote about, in remaining "a little boy"; but financial success and disheartenment about human folly as a result of the war caused him to grow up; and, as Merlin predicted, when he no longer reached for the moon, he no longer caught fireflies. It seems very likely that the puzzling "moon" of the title of *The Moon is Down* may be Steinbeck's vision of the human potentiality for greatness.

Steinbeck may have been content to cease being a little boy. He spoke in one of the rare flashes of his old manner in *Sweet Thursday* of "the hopeless wish of a man wanting to be a little boy, forgetting the pain of little boys." Perhaps he no longer wished to endure pain, forgetting that the pain of children is a sign of growth and that without it there may may be no consciousness of growth—nor even any growth. His lashing the critics in his defense of *Burning Bright* and his angry satire in *Sweet Thursday* suggest a man furious at the pain inflicted by those who were only trying to make him see what had happened to him. To summarize, Steinbeck, although he had abandoned his own countryside for the city, lacked the sophistication to deal with urban society as he had with rural.

There are slender evidences, however, that Steinbeck may have arrested his descent. I cannot agree with Peter Lisca that his most recent novel, *The Short Reign of Pippin IV*, is interesting only as evidence of the author's decline; it represents, I believe, a perceptible change for the better.

Lisca reports that Steinbeck was surprised when the Book-of-the-Month Club selected this novel, since he thought its appeal would be extremely limited. It is hard to see why he thought so. The fable of the man who rejects high public office—in *Pippin*, the kingship of France—rather than compromise his integrity by failing to tell the truth is one of the oldest and most popular in Western literature.

The story can be traced back to Plato's account of Socrates' "Apology," but it is surely much older. Shakespeare used it in *Coriolanus*, and it was a favorite of early American Federalists like Hugh Henry Brackenridge (*Modern Chivalry*) and James Fenimore Cooper. It was freely exploited in the thirties not only by George Kaufman and Moss Hart in the enormously popular *You Can't Take It With You,* but several times by Frank Capra in much admired idealistic film comedies like *Mr. Deeds Goes to Town* and *Mr. Smith Goes to Washington.* At the time Steinbeck's novel appeared, one of the most popular contemporary English novels was an academic version of the same story, Kingsley Amis's *Lucky Jim.* As this list suggests, the legends of the man who preferred truth to power has been to the intellectual what the Cinderella myth has been to the anti-intellectual.

Actually there is much of Steinbeck himself in Pippin. It is hard to believe it entirely coincidental that Pippin is exactly the age—fifty-four—Steinbeck must have been when he began work on the novel; there is no reason to think that Steinbeck did not also suppose himself, "lean, handsome, and healthy." It is even more significant that Pippin, living in Paris as Steinbeck often does, derives his income from the "eastward-facing slopes" of some hills on the Loire, where his vineyards produce a wine that does not "travel well." Steinbeck himself came from a fertile valley with mountains to the west, and he had been deriving his income from an artistic product of this soil that he had begun to find did not travel well.

There may even be further parallels in the story. Pippin reluctantly consents to be a "patsy" in order to provide the French the leader they think they want; but when he discovers that their selfishness and greed are responsible for their troubles, he tells them the truth, gives up his office, and returns home to spend his time as an amateur astronomer gazing at the stars. It would not be hard to see these events as mirroring Steinbeck's own career. When he had told the truth in such novels as *In Dubious Battle* and *The Grapes of Wrath,* he had been bitterly attacked. When he tried to write what he thought the public wanted in *East of Eden* and *Sweet Thursday,* he had not attracted enough public support to compensate for the loss of critical esteem. Perhaps he decided it was time to stop trying either to demand action or to please a fickle public and to start gazing at the stars, as his character Pippin does after abdicating. He concludes in *Pippin,* as he had in *Cannery Row,* that man's hope lies not in courting the mob or getting placed at the California Institute of Technology, but in the solace of detached study.

Steinbeck's reservations about the potential audience for Pippin may also have been caused by skepticism about the market for city novels, about his being accepted as an urban novelist, or about the readers' perception of the point that the individual's salvation lies in creative detachment (they had certainly missed this idea in *Cannery Row*).

As for the first two doubts, although Steinbeck might have failed, the odds rather favor urban novels. Long the predominant form in England, many examples of the *genre* have succeeded financially in America. If few have been critically acclaimed, the fault could lie with writers who are not sufficiently perceptive of the complexities of city life. It is doubtful, despite the wishful thinking of agrarian conservatives and the uneasy urban-rural compromise of the post-war subdivision, whether the soil holds its old spell for American readers. Our country is becoming increasingly urbanized, and we are being forced to recognize the fact artistically and politically.

Of course, Steinbeck himself may still harbor the preconception that the American Everyman dreams like the Joads in *The Grapes of Wrath* of "a little white cottage" in the country. There is no reason, however, why others should not have been "converted" to the city as, in "The Making of a New Yorker," Steinbeck explains he was. Perhaps the response to Pippin should have surprisingly proved to its author—as "La Santa Roja's" reaction did to Henry Morgan in *Cup of Gold*— that he was not so different from others as he would have liked to suppose.

Steinbeck's failure to put across his points in his previous novels may be attributable simply to his audience's not reading carefully enough to realize that a complex and subtle novel like *Cannery Row* was written in praise of detachment. When in *Burning Bright*, Steinbeck had stated his thesis so explicitly that no one could mistake it, it was not the idea but the lack of any flavor of recognizable life that left readers unimpressed. In *Pippin*, Steinbeck avoided both extremes: the characters are not so special as those in *Cannery Row* but are more convincing than the thinly fleshed abstractions in *Burning Bright*. The reader who thinks of himself as an ordinary individual, but who yearns for power he feels he would wield wisely, can readily identify himself with Pippin and learn with him that power and prestige are not worth the compromise of personal integrity they entail. Steinbeck had at last found how to say simply and unmistakably what he had long sought to say. Although Pippin is not sufficiently distinctive in thesis or structure to be outstanding art, it is something that no other Steinbeck novel had been since *Cannery Row*—an auspicious omen.

One heartening characteristic of *Pippin* is that in this first urban novel Steinbeck begins to solve some problems that he had failed to solve during his lean years. He comes up in *Pippin* against the same problem that had baffled him in *East of Eden*: Why do people hurt others? Again he rejects teleological solutions. Pippin meets an old man who is one of the kind that "pulls things out"—like Juan Chicoy in *The Wayward Bus*. When Pippin asks him why some people do good and some bad, the old man only replies helplessly, as Casy did in *The Grapes of Wrath*, "I don't understand. . . . There's just people—just what people do."

Perhaps people just do what they like. The transcendental concept that they might like to do good rather than evil is the point of the "Code Pippin" that the king describes in the catastrophic speech that tumbles him from the throne. What the seven points of the code boil down to is a demand for equal opportunity for all. Rather than being enthusiastic about these proposals or outraged by them, the people are simply stunned. No individual can entertain the thought of changes that might end his self-assumed monopoly on human dignity. Because of what Steinbeck describes as "their own deep sense of guilt" (*difference* would be a more appropriate non-teleological term than *guilt*), they mock and finally overthrow Pippin.

The novel shows again, as *The Wayward Bus* had, that Steinbeck cannot quite square his non-teleological observation that people are simply what they are with his transcendental desire that they improve themselves. He has still not decided whether his primary allegiance is to science or satire. But in Pippin he comes closer than in any of his previous books to recognizing that since men are what they are, they must become conscious of their present status and change, if they can at all, after recognizing where they are starting from —without feeling the overwhelming guilt about being different that embarrasses them and causes, for example, the listeners to Pippin's speech to relieve their tensions by breaking into hysterical laughter when they discover his robes do not fit. The end of the book indicates, like the endings of *The Grapes of Wrath* and *Cannery Row*, that conditions might improve if men would simply be content to accept themselves as they are—not to cease trying to change themselves but to stop persecuting others for being different from them. Again, however, Steinbeck refuses to express any fatuous hope that most men will achieve this position. What he has done is learn to perceive in larger terms—the corporation and the nation—the same things that he had earlier perceived in terms of relatively homogeneous groups within his native state.

If Steinbeck could find dramatically effective ways to express these larger perceptions, he could once again write distinguished books that did not simply repeat his earlier works, for one shortcoming of American literature in the twentieth century has been that few writers have been able to understand and discuss human problems in terms of the large-scale social units into which men are principally organized today. A reviewer for the *New Yorker* (June 25, 1960) discussing some of Ezra Pound's collected exhortations points out that "any community larger and less organic than an American town in 1750 baffles and enrages him." This perceptive statement could be made of many of our contemporary American authors, and the applicability of this remark is an indication of just how far they lag behind our technicians, who have not quite kept pace with the city, but who are at least beginning to catch up with it. Chester E. Eisinger points out, in the *University of Kansas City Review* (Autumn, 1947) in one of the most thoughtful criticisms of *The Grapes of Wrath*, the anachronism today of the Jeffersonian concept of every free man as an owner of agricultural land, where he could enjoy the unrestricted development of his individualism; but such thinking still abounds in our creative writing.

If Steinbeck could shuck off his country-boy manner and bring the same skills to the portrayal of the city that he once did to that of the country, he might become an even more significant writer than he has been, because a truly "contemporary" writer must be able to exploit artistically urban culture. "Slum" novelists like James T. Farrell and Nelson Algren do not necessarily have a thorough grasp of urban culture, for the slum is not the metropolis but a rather primitive enclave within it. These writers are more likely to be akin to a rural writer like Erskine Caldwell than they are to a writer like J. D. Salinger, who perceives that the city poses our problems even if he sees little hope of solving them.

Another work of Steinbeck's that indicates ability to handle the urban scene and that is a hopeful harbinger is a short story published in the *Atlantic Monthly* in 1956, "How Mr. Hogan Robbed a Bank."[2] In this, one of the few short stories he has written in the last twenty years, he succeeds in doing several things that he had not done before. First, he achieves the non-teleological viewpoint he has long sought; there are no indications of Hogan's motives for robbing the bank except his curiosity to see if it could be done without a lot of "hanky-panky"; his motive is, therefore, artistic not social.

Yet the story is not mere reporting. Without an editorial word, Steinbeck produces an ironic, final twist by having Hogan, who has just successfully robbed the bank, reward his two children—one of whom has just won a prize in the Hearst "Why I Like America" contest—for their virtues with two five-dollar bills from the loot. It is also obvious that Hogan has been able to carry off the robbery because of his observation of the bank employees' unvarying routine. Steinbeck is again satirizing the dangers of getting into a rut.

What is important, however, is that in this story Steinbeck makes a bank both a thoroughly human institution and an object of ridicule. The attitude is far from that expressed in *The Grapes of Wrath*, in which the author fears the ruthless impersonality of the bank almost as much as his share-cropping characters. Steinbeck is now able not just to say that urban life is ridiculous, but to show that it is. Although we have had many melodramas of city life, we have had few comedies, because few writers since Dickens have understood the complexities of urban life well enough to demonstrate convincingly that the individual can get the better of that monster that crushes individuality—the city. In "How Mr. Hogan Robbed a Bank," Steinbeck shows the individual triumphing; and, fusing narrative and allegory for the first time since *Cannery Row*, he does so in a story containing convincingly real people and not a word of editorial explanation.

It is discouraging to find that four years have produced no successor to this story. It seems unlikely that Steinbeck, no longer young, will be able to exploit his new subject as he did the old; he has, however, at least begun to move up from the low-water mark of his career, *Sweet Thursday*. Even if he does not continue to write so successfully about urban man as he has about rural, he has pointed out a path others might profitably follow.

I cannot agree with those who would write Steinbeck off as not even a serious writer. His failures by no means cancel out his successes. The author of *The Pastures of Heaven, Tortilla Flat, In Dubious Battle, Of Mice and Men, The Red Pony, The Grapes of Wrath, Cannery Row*, and a dozen distinguished short stories cannot fail to occupy a high place among contemporary American writers. Nor can we safely assume that he will produce, or at least inspire, no more successes. The answer to the question "What happened to John Steinbeck?" is that although, like our literature generally, he is not in top form because he has had to adjust to a new environment, he is still around.

Notes and References

Chapter One

1. *New York Times Magazine*, Part II, pp. 26-27, February 1, 1953. For a special issue commemorating the tercentenary of municipal self-government in New York City, Steinbeck wrote these memoirs of the visits that led to his settling in the city as a representative of others who had been attracted there from the hinterland.

2. "The Secret Weapon We Were Afraid to Use," *Collier's*, CXXXI, 9-13, January 10, 1953. Steinbeck recounts other troubles with bureaucrats during the war in "About Ed Ricketts," the preface to *The Log from the Sea of Cortez* (New York, 1951).

Chapter Two

1. Gannett gives this figure in his preface to the first reprinting of *Cup of Gold* (Covici, Friede, 1936) after the success of *Tortilla Flat* had created a market for Steinbeck's hitherto obscure, earlier works.

Chapter Six

1. The "double-edged" metaphor suggests some particularly intriguing comparisons between this novel and the second book of the *Morte d'Arthur*, the story of Balin, "the knight of the dolorous stroke," who carries a two-edged blade. This ambitious and virtuous young recruit to the Round Table is killed at an early age in hand-to-hand combat with his brother, who is also inadvertently slain.

Chapter Nine

1. A number of novelists and non-fiction writers, especially patriotic Californians, were stung into attempting to refute Steinbeck. Peter Lisca discusses several of their works in *The Wide World of John Steinbeck*, pp. 149-51. The least volatile is A. I. Bezzerides' novel, *There is a Happy Land* (New York, 1942). The most consequential, and the one that best shows why these works failed to make as great an impression as Steinbeck's, is the novel

Of Human Kindness (New York, 1940), a quasi-official answer of the Associated Farmers by Ruth Comfort Mitchell (pseudonym of Mrs. W. S. Young, writer of several novels for popular consumption). The defects of her work, which makes the emotionally charged *The Grapes of Wrath* appear objective by contrast, are analyzed by Carey McWilliams in *New Republic,* CIII, 125 (July 22, 1940).

2. Magny, Claude-Edmonde, "Steinbeck, or The Limits of the Impersonal Novel," in Tedlock and Wicker, *Steinbeck and His Critics,* pp. 216-27, translated by Françoise Gourier from *L'Age du Roman Américain.*

Chapter Ten

1. In an attempt to give his story universal significance, Steinbeck refuses to speak of Germans and Norwegians; but this somewhat Jamesian device only confuses matters because of remarks like this one of Mayor Orden's to Colonel Lanser: "In all the world yours is the only government and people with a record of defeat after defeat for centuries and every time because you did not understand people." If this statement does not refer to the Germans, it does not make sense at all; and if the German attitude is really unique, the situation cannot be "universalized."

2. His views are amplified, but the situation is not clarified in the play. The suspicion that he is an opportunist seeking to exploit the credulous masses is only further confirmed when he tells Mayor Orden's friend Dr. Winter that "The democracy was rotten and inefficient. Things will be better now. . . . When you understand the new order you will know I am right."

Chapter Thirteen

1. Seixas, Antonia, "John Steinbeck and the Non-Teleological Bus," *Steinbeck and His Critics,* edited by F. W. Tedlock, Jr., and C. V. Wicker (Albuquerque, 1957), pp. 275-80. Since Miss Seixas was at one time Steinbeck's secretary, her article affords an unusual insight into the author's intentions.

2. *Saturday Review of Literature,* XXXIII, 20-21 (November 11, 1950).

3. Exactly what the word means is one of the "problems" facing the characters in the novel. An unlikely group of Chinese savants study Hebrew in order to decide whether it means "Thou shalt," as it is translated in the King James version, or "Do thou," as in the American Standard version. These sages decide it means "thou mayest" and this interpretation endows man with free will.

Chapter Fourteen

1. "Rationale," *Steinbeck and His Critics*, edited by E. W. Tedlock, Jr., and C. V. Wicker (Albuquerque, 1957), pp. 308-9.

2. The University of Texas has also acquired a manuscript of a work entitled "How Mr. Hogan Robbed a Bank or The American Dream," described by the author on the cover as "an unpublished, unproduced, unconsidered play in one act" (F. Warren Roberts, "The D. H. Lawrence New Mexico Fellowship Fund Collection," *Texas Quarterly*, III, 215 [Summer, 1960]). If Steinbeck has dramatized the story, the play version is not publicly available.

Selected Bibliography

THE WRITINGS OF JOHN STEINBECK

Only the most important works are mentioned. For a more extensive but not definitive bibliography see Peter Lisca, *The Wide World of John Steinbeck*.

COLLECTIONS

The Portable Steinbeck, selected by Pascal Covici, Enlarged Edition, New York: The Viking Press, 1946, contains an introduction by Lewis Gannett that is one of the most valuable pieces of Steinbeck criticism available, as well as six short stories, two complete novels, and excerpts from nine other books.

The Short Novels of John Steinbeck, introduced by Joseph Henry Jackson, New York: The Viking Press, 1953, contains *Tortilla Flat*, *Of Mice and Men*, *The Red Pony*, *The Moon is Down*, *Cannery Row*, and *The Pearl*.

BOOKS

Bombs Away, New York: The Viking Press, 1942.

Burning Bright, New York: The Viking Press, 1950.

Cannery Row, New York: The Viking Press, 1945; Bantam Books (paperbound), 1947.

Cup of Gold, New York: Robert M. McBride & Co., 1929; Covici, Friede, 1936.

East of Eden, New York: The Viking Press, 1952; Bantam Books (paperbound), 1955.

The Forgotten Village, New York: The Viking Press, 1941, contains scenes from the documentary film made in Mexico by Herbert Kline.

The Grapes of Wrath, New York: The Viking Press, 1939; Modern Library, 1941; Bantam Books (paperbound), 1945; Compass Books (paperbound), 1958. The film script by Nunnally Johnson is in *Twenty Best Film Plays*, edited by John Gassner and Dudely Nichols, New York: Crown, 1943.

In Dubious Battle, New York: Covici, Friede, 1936; Modern Library, 1939.

The Log from the Sea of Cortez, New York: The Viking Press, 1951, contains "About Ed Ricketts," a valuable biographical sketch of Steinbeck's friend, and the text of *Sea of Cortez*, originally published in 1941.

The Long Valley, New York: The Viking Press, 1948; Compass Books (paperbound), 1956.

The Moon is Down (novel), New York: The Viking Press, 1942.

The Moon is Down (play), New York: The Viking Press, 1942; abridged in *The Best Plays of 1941-1942*, edited by Burns Mantle (New York, 1942), pp. 72-108.

Of Mice and Men (novel), New York: Covici, Friede, 1937; Modern Library, 1938; Bantam Classics (paperbound), 1955.

Of Mice and Men (play), New York: Covici, Friede, 1937; abridged in *The Best Plays of 1937-1938*, edited by Burns Mantle (New York, 1938), pp. 31-66.

Once There Was a War, New York: The Viking Press, 1958, collects Steinbeck's wartime dispatches to the New York *Herald Tribune*.

The Pastures of Heaven, New York: Brewer, Warren & Putnam, 1932; Covici, Friede, 1935; Bantam Books (paperbound), 1951.

The Pearl, New York: The Viking Press, 1947.

The Red Pony, New York: Covici, Friede, 1937 (limited, signed edition); illustrated by Wesley Dennis, New York: The Viking Press, 1945; Bantam Books (paperbound), 1948.

A Russian Journal, with photographs by Robert Capa, New York: The Viking Press, 1948.

Sainty Katy, the Virgin, New York: Covici, Friede, 1936 (limited, signed edition).

The Short Reign of Pippin IV, New York: The Viking Press, 1957; Bantam Books (paperbound), 1958.

Sweet Thursday, New York: The Viking Press, 1954.

Their Blood is Strong, San Francisco: Simon J. Lubin Society of California, Inc. (paperbound), 1938, contains articles on conditions among the migrant laborers in California originally printed in the San Francisco *News* in October, 1936, and an epilogue written in 1938.

To a God Unknown, New York: Robert O. Ballou, 1933; Covici, Friede, 1935; Bantam Books (paperbound), 1955.

Tortilla Flat, New York: Covici, Friede, 1935; Modern Library, 1937; Penguin Books (paperbound), 1946.

The Wayward Bus, New York: The Viking Press, 1947.

* * *

Selected Bibliography

Pipe Dream, by Oscar Hammerstein II and Richard Rodgers, New York: The Viking Press, 1954, is a musical comedy based on Sweet Thursday.

UNCOLLECTED PIECES

"His Father" (short story), Reader's Digest, LV, 19-21 (September, 1949).

"How Mr. Hogan Robbed a Bank" (short story), Atlantic Monthly, CXCVII, 58-61 (March, 1956).

"How to Tell Good Guys from Bad Guys" (essay), The Reporter, XII, 42-44 (March 10, 1955), is a satire on McCarthyism and television stereotypes that has been frequently reprinted.

"I Go Back to Ireland" (autobiography), Collier's, CXXXI, 48-50 (January 31, 1953), describes a visit to his maternal grandfather's home town of Ballydally.

"Making of a New Yorker" (autobiography), New York Times Magazine, Part II, pp. 26-27 (February 1, 1953).

"The Miracle of Tepayac" (short story), Collier's, CXXII, 22-23 (December 25, 1948).

"A Plea to Teachers" (essay), Saturday Review, XXXVIII, 24 (April 30, 1955), counsels against asking students to write letters of inquiry to authors.

"The Secret Weapon We Were Afraid to Use" (autobiography), Collier's, CXXXI, 9-13 (January 10, 1953), describes a scheme to help the Allies win World War II.

"The Time the Wolves Ate the Vice Principal" (short story), '47, The Magazine of the Year, I, 26-27 (March, 1947), is described by Peter Lisca as an inter-chapter omitted from Cannery Row.

RECORDING

The only commercial recording of Steinbeck reading from his own works was issued as a part of the out-of-print Columbia Literary Series (SL-190). On a single disc, he reads "The Snake" and "Johnny Bear" from The Long Valley (Columbia, ML-4756).

WRITINGS ABOUT STEINBECK

BOOKS

LISCA, PETER. The Wide World of John Steinbeck (New Brunswick, New Jersey; 1958), the most comprehensive scholarly study of Steinbeck, primarily concerns the structural and linguistic qualities of the novel and attempts by close reading to rectify shortcomings of previous criticisms.

MOORE, HARRY THORNTON. *The Novels of John Steinbeck, A First Study* (Chicago, 1939), a pioneering study of "the poet of the dispossessed," is still a valuable source of biographical and bibliographical information.

TEDLOCK, E. W., JR., and C. V. WICKER, editors. *Steinbeck and His Critics, A Record of Twenty-Five Years* (Albuquerque, New Mexico; 1957), is an indispensable guide to Steinbeck studies containing an introductory survey of the criticism by the editors, a "literary biography" by Peter Lisca, six critical pieces by Steinbeck, and twenty-two critical essays by seventeen writers.

ESSAYS

Only the most valuable essays which are *not* included in Tadlock and Wicker's compilation are described here. Consult the annual American bibliographies in *PMLA* for further criticisms.

ANGOFF, ALLEN (editor). *American Writing Today* (New York, 1957) pp. 398-99, reprints the review from the London *Times Literary Supplement*, September 9, 1939, pointing out the difference between Steinbeck's and other writers' approach to the problems of the American west.

BAKER, CARLOS. "*In Dubious Battle* Revalued," *New York Times Book Review*, July 5, 1943, pp. 4, 16, lauds the novel as an allegory of failures of human reason attributable to bionomic (ecological) unknowns.

BLUESTONE, GEORGE. *Novels into Films* (Baltimore, 1957), pp. 147-69, compares Nunnally Johnson's film script to the novel and elucidates the meaning of the original by analyzing the "sweetening" of the end of the film.

CALVERTON, V. F. "Steinbeck, Hemingway, and Faulkner," *Modern Quarterly*, XI, 36-44 (February, 1939), contrasts Faulkner's pessimistic with Steinbeck's optimistic views about oppressed people.

CHAMPNEY, FREEMAN. "Critics in Search of an Author," *Antioch Review*, XVIII, 371-75 (Fall, 1958), observes that Steinbeck's diversity and touchiness may indicate an insecurity about the relationship of an artist to his audience and his culture.

EISINGER, CHESTER E. "Jeffersonian Agrarianism in *The Grapes of Wrath*," *University of Kansas City Review*, XIV, 149-54 (Autumn, 1947), shows the influence of Jeffersonian agrarian thought· on Steinbeck's thinking and the anachronism of such thinking in an increasingly industrialized society.

FRENCH, WARREN G. "Another Look at *The Grapes of Wrath*," *Colorado Quarterly*, III, 337-43 (Winter, 1955) answers Bernard Bowron's charge in "*The Grapes of Wrath*: A 'Waggons Westward' Romance" (*Colorado Quarterly*, III, 84-91, Summer, 1954) that the novel is "literary engineering" by pointing out that the Mosaic exodus provides a more likely analogue than the "Covered Wagon" romance.

FROHOCK, W. M. "John Steinbeck—The Utility of Wrath," *Novel of Violence in America*, Revised Edition (Dallas, 1958), pp. 124-43, argues that the strong emotions Steinbeck needs to hold his· post-war novels together are. lacking.

GEISMAR, MAXWELL. "John Steinbeck: Of Wrath of Joy," *Writers in Crisis, The American Novel: 1925-1940* (Boston, 1942), pp. 237-70, one of the most readable and perceptive accounts of Steinbeck's early works, argues that the author considers civilization as the source of man's troubles and reflects the "evasions of his generation."

————. *American Moderns from Rebellion to Conformity* (New York, 1958), pp. 151-56, 164-67, laments the increasing trickiness and theatricality of Steinbeck's post-war work.

GIERASCH, WALTER. "Steinbeck's 'The Red Pony II: The Great Mountains,'" *Explicator*, Vol. IV, Item 39 (March, 1946), explains the way in which Steinbeck uses the story to show Jody's learning of the mystery and inevitability of death.

GROMMON, ALFRED H. "Who is 'The Leader of the People'? Helping Students Examine Fiction," *English Journal*, XVIII, 449-61, 476 (November, 1959), is a detailed and convincing analysis of Carl Tiflin as a teleological thinker and Jody as a non-teleologist and future "leader of the people."

JONES, CLAUDE E. "Proletarian Writing and John Steinbeck," *Sewanee Review*, XLVIII, 445-56 (October, 1940), explains that Steinbeck is not a Marxist, but unconvincingly insists that his novels treat local problems without universal implications.

JONES, WILLIAM M. "Steinbeck's 'Flight,'" *Explicator*, Vol. XVIII, Item 11 (November, 1959), is a questionable interpretation of the story as an allegory of a flight from conformity to non-conformity.

KAZIN, ALFRED. *On Native Grounds*, Anchor Books Edition (New York, 1956), pp. 304-10, written from a sophisticated urban viewpoint, finds Steinbeck's naturalism refreshing but incompletely human because the author's preoccupation with simple people prevents his realizing the complexity of modern life.

LEWIS, RICHARD W. B. "John Steinbeck: The Fitful Daemon," *The Young Rebel in American Literature*, edited by Carl Bode (London, 1959), pp. 121-41, questions whether Steinbeck is still an important writer and attributes his decline to his inability to believe that there is anything really wrong with the human heart.

METZGER, CHARLES R. "Steinbeck's Version of the Pastoral," *Modern Fiction Studies*, VI, 115-24 (Summer, 1960), ingeniously links *Sweet Thursday* with the pastoral tradition but ignores the novel's anti-intellectualism.

POLLOCK, THEODORE. "On the Ending of *The Grapes of Wrath*," *Modern Fiction Studies*, IV, 177-8 (Summer, 1958), argues impressively that the novel is well designed and essentially optimistic.

POWELL, LAWRENCE CLARK. "Toward a Bibliography of John Steinbeck," *Colophon*, New Series, III, 558-68 (Autumn, 1938), contains valuable biographical and bibliographical information acquired by the distinguished librarian who was one of the earliest Steinbeck collectors.

PRESCOTT, ORVILLE. "Squandered Talents," *In My Opinion* (Indianapolis, 1952), pp. 58-64, is one of the bitterest attacks in print upon the kind of people Steinbeck writes about in *Cannery Row*.

RICHARDS, EDMUND C. "The Challenge of John Steinbeck," *North American Review*, CCXLIII, 406-13 (Summer, 1937), defends—in the first magazine to print Steinbeck's short stories —the author against "bloodless moralists" and praises his refusal to limit his vision and his resistance to the "dry rot of gentility."

STRAUMANN, HEINRICH. *American Literature in the Twentieth Century* (London, 1951), pp. 107-11, explains European admiration for *The Moon is Down* and the emphasis upon non-material values, especially the dignity of the individual, in Steinbeck's work generally.

TAYLOR, WALTER FULLER. "*The Grapes of Wrath* Reconsidered," *Mississippi Quarterly*, XII, 136-44 (Summer, 1959), is a careful and thorough elucidation of the shortcomings of the novel from a conservative Christian viewpoint.

WALCUTT, CHARLES C. *American Literary Naturalism* (Minneapolis, 1956), pp. 258-70, one of the keenest analyses of Steinbeck's later novels, points out that the author's work is an advance over earlier naturalistic writing because of his use of traditional forms to strengthen the presentation of nebulous idealism.

WEEKS, DONALD. "Steinbeck Against Steinbeck," *Pacific Spectator,* I, 447-57 (Autumn, 1947), complains that Steinbeck's increasing sentimentality may be the result of his not understanding the relationship of non-teleological thought to his art.

WEST, RAY B., JR. *The Short Story in America* (Chicago, 1952), pp. 45-51, discusses "The Chrysanthemums" as a celebration of natural instinct in which irony holds sentimentality in check.

WILSON, EDMUND. "The Boys in the Back Room," *Classics and Commercials* (New York, 1950), pp. 35-45, source of the much-quoted criticism of Steinbeck's "animalizing" humanity, objects to the author's biological preoccupations but commends his "unpanicky scrutiny of life."

Index

Names of characters and places in Steinbeck's novels and other fiction are followed by the title—in parentheses—of the work in which they appear.